"Why You Need To Be The Man"

"Why You Need To Be The Man"

Samuel L. Digby

Copyright © 2010 by Samuel L. Digby.

Library of Congress Control Number:		2010908548
ISBN:	Hardcover	978-1-4535-1996-7
	Softcover	978-1-4535-1995-0
	Ebook	978-1-4535-1997-4

All rights reserved. No part of this book may be reproduced or transmitted in any form or by any means, electronic or mechanical, including photocopying, recording, or by any information storage and retrieval system, without permission in writing from the copyright owner.

Bible verses were taken from the King James Version Copyright 1994

This book was printed in the United States of America.

To order additional copies of this book, contact:
Xlibris Corporation
1-888-795-4274
www.Xlibris.com
Orders@Xlibris.com
76282

Contents

Acknowledgments 9

Introduction 11

Chapter 1   Back In The Day 23

Chapter 2   Don't Talk About It; Be About It 33

Chapter 3   All Eyes On You 49

Chapter 4   The Three Ds Of Manhood 61

Chapter 5   Don't Be A Victim 78

Chapter 6   Don't Listen To That Woman When She Says 82

Chapter 7   Find Your Niche & Work It 89

Chapter 8   Know Where Your Strength Comes From 107

Chapter 9   When All Else Fails, Keep On Trying 115

Index 119

To Brandi

It was great having you in class.

"God bless
Keep the faith"

Sam Digby

This book is dedicated to the memory of my parents

*Mr. Samuel L. Digby Sr.
and
Mrs. Joyce M. Digby*

Acknowledgments

First I have to give thanks to the almighty God for making this project possible. I thank God for putting the right words in my spirit to put on paper so that this project can be a blessing to someone else.

Thank you, Mom and Dad, for the work that you put into me and our family. I know at times it was not easy, but you stayed the course and fought a good fight. I miss both of you so very much, but I know that God had a much bigger plan for you than I could ever imagine. God bless both of you and I hope that you guys are looking down on us from the heavens above with a smile. Until we meet again, I love you . . .

Robert L. Digby, thank you for your encouraging words and powerful insight. I never would have even considered the law enforcement profession if it were not for you. You first introduced to me the difference I could make in my community through public service. I wish you were still here in the physical sense to see this project unfold, but I know you are now with my parents and I'm sure that all of you are celebrating in a heavenly way. I will never forget you. Thanks again for all you have done for our family. The legacy you left will continue on.

Uncle Stratton Knight, you have guided me spiritually for over thirty years. God bless you and Progressive MB Church. Thank you for your wisdom and knowledge and may you continue to do God's work ever so well.

Reverend James E. Walker (International Church of Prayer) thank you for your spiritual guidance, while I was a child. You gave me my first job outside of the home in the church. Thank you for the letters of recommendations for school and eulogizing both of my parents. You will always hold a special place in my heart. I would not be in the position I am in now, if it were not for you and the ICP church family.

Former Dallas Police Chief David Kunkle, thank you for your leadership and the role you played in my professional development. I wish you success in your future endeavors, and it was indeed a pleasure serving under your leadership.

Dallas Police Assistant Chief Daniel V. Garcia, thank you for your wisdom and feedback while I prepared this manuscript.

Dallas Police Sgt. Preston K. Gilstrap, you have been a warrior for fighting social injustice for a long time. Keep up the good work and don't retire just yet. God still has more work for you to do in our communities. Thank you for mentoring me and for your positive words of encouragement. Thank you for being a true leader that we all have been able to count on for over thirty years.

Dr. Roy Alston, your dedication and wisdom has inspired me to want to achieve greatness. I have listened to you even when you did not know I was listening. Your school of thought on policing and manhood are felt well beyond the perimeters of the community you serve. Thank you for being a true friend and sharing some positive insight with me on this project. You have a precious gift and are indeed a true leader.

I want to say thanks to the entire AME church family which has provided a balance in my life over the last seven years. Pastor Kenneth Robinson of St. Andrew AME and Pastor Juan Tolliver of St. Paul AME, may God continue to bless each one of you and see favor.

I want to say thanks to all of my primary and elementary school teachers who educated me along the way. If not for a teacher, where would any of us be?

I want to say thanks to all the people that I left out who lived in the communities that were instrumental in my growth and development. Please understand me when I say, "You are appreciated."

I want to say thanks to Faith Go, the submission and editing staff, and the interior design staff at Xlibris Publishing. You guys spent hours making sure that this project came to life.

Thanks to my wife, Jacqueline, and our children whom have been a consistent source of strength and inspiration.

Introduction

The year is 2009, and I think back over the course of my life and I remember how things once were. I think back to where I came from to where I am today. I am very fortunate to be in the position that I am in today. Today, I can stand tall and truthfully say that there is a God who cares about each and every one of His children because I am a living witness. It is truly by God's grace that each and every one of us has made it this far. And only God's grace will determine how much further we go.

I think back about some of the guys that I grew up with in my old neighborhood. Some of them are dead, some went to jail, and there were a few guys who ended up doing really well for themselves. I think back about all the things that I have done, places I have been, and people I have hung around. I know deep down in my spirit that I had a whole lot of people praying for me. The funny thing about being a kid is that you think that you are invincible. I know this is exactly how I felt. Think back for a moment when you were a kid. Think back to when you did not know the definition of danger. My mother used to call this "tombstone" courage.

Tombstone Courage

Tombstone courage was more prominent in little boys than in little girls. At least that appeared to be the case thirty years ago. Today, girls are committing the same types of crimes that boys commit. Tombstone courage exists when nothing else around you matters and you are willing to take that chance.

Generally, children don't think rationally especially young boys. When lack of rationality is mixed with aggression, this can consequently equal tombstone courage. As we get older and gain more life experience, tombstone courage should decrease, and we should become a little more stable minded.

Can you imagine coming face-to-face with a kid who has tombstone courage? This is the type of kid who will do or say anything. They have no regard for their own life, let alone someone else's. The true tragedy is carrying this over into adulthood. This explains why a twenty-one-year-old young person will go out in the streets and cut somebody's arm off to take a watch and pawn it for $200. To normal people, this makes no sense. To a person who has the idea in their head that the world owes him something, this is just another walk in the park.

As young boys, we are conditioned to be aggressive and not show off our emotions as much as little girls. I can remember as a little boy, I could never come home crying to my parents about what some kid did to me in the streets. When I was eight years old, I remember getting into a mutual fight with a kid down the street from my house. At the time, I was living on the South Side (Chicago). Kids in that neighborhood exploited weaknesses of the other children. Chicago was not the easiest city to grow up in. I remember counting at least two to three fights everyday, walking to and from school. I remember one day I came home crying to my mother about being in a fight. My mother made me dry my face and sent me back outside. She told me that it was OK to lose a fight and live to fight another day. But under no circumstances could I run from a mutual fight and expect the person whom I ran from to respect me in the future. My mother was not a violent person; however, she did stand for what she believed in. I did what my mother said, and even though I lost the fight, the other kid knew that I was not a pushover. Twenty years later, we still are the best of friends.

Boys will try things that most girls will only laugh at. If you don't think this is the case, maybe you need to look at the penal institutions in the United States. Males represent the largest number of incarceration of the two sexes by a long shot. As a young kid you think nothing out there in the streets can harm you. I had ice water running through my veins as did most of the kids in my neighborhood. This was the tombstone courage talking again. I did not put a lot of stock in the dangers that existed when I was hanging out in the streets. This did not bother me at all. But as my father always told me, "Son, keep on living." What my father was trying to get me to understand, was that if I keep on living, I will keep on learning and I will understand the dangers in the world that are viewed from the eyes of a parent.

A Parent Who is Present or Absent

I was blessed with good fortune to have a strong family foundation. I had both Momma and Daddy in the home. As a matter of fact, most of the kids on my block had both parents in the home. Now, I want to be clear. Having two parents in the home does not guarantee anything. I knew several kids on the block that had both parents in the home and either one or both parents were absentee. Absentee meaning, they were physically in the home, but socially and emotionally detached from the home. Having an absentee parent is almost as bad as not having a parent at all. I will say that having two parents in my home proved to be a valuable asset for me growing up. As a child, I learned best by being "hands-on" and being observant.

I was never a troublesome kid. As a matter of fact, I was often too scared to do anything that would get me into trouble. My father made sure that even if I were not afraid of anyone, I would be afraid of him. This kept me in check. How many children in this world today don't fear their parents? I personally believe that this is the problem. Now I don't condone abusing children. But, I am an advocate of parents being actively involved in the lives of their children and making themselves available to deal with the problems that may arise.

In my house, Daddy ruled. Daddy made the rules, and he enforced them. As I look back, this was not that bad a system. My father was not an absentee parent. I truly believe that a child who does not fear his/her parents does not know that his/her parents are capable of doing anything. I feared my dad to the point of what I knew he was capable of doing to me, if I were caught doing wrong. Some people may call this controlling, but I call it parenting. You must be harder on boys than on girls. It takes a man to teach a boy how to be a man.

My father was like the legislative and executive branches of government put together in one. When I saw trouble coming my way, I was always good about avoiding it and letting my friends tell me all about it the next day at school.

The Real Police

I respected authority. I think this is one of the greatest gifts any parents can give their children. If a child does not do what their parents say, when they become adults and get into trouble they will do what the police say. The first authority figures I learned to respect were my parents. I thank God for blessing me with parents that taught me about authority and how to respect it. You can never underestimate the importance of respecting and obeying authority. My house was like a little city and my dad was the sheriff. This type of environment proved to be beneficial in my development, because it taught me how to deal with authoritative figures as an adult. People who lack the skills in learning how to be submissive to those in charge usually have a hard life. There are times when you need to stand your ground and stand for what is right. The key, however, is to be old enough to accept the responsibilities that go with the decisions you make. Who really likes being told what to do when they feel like they can make their own decisions? There were plenty of times I wanted to do what I felt I wanted to do, however, my father had other ideas.

I drew a fine line between being mischievous and outright crazy. Children can do some really dumb things. This is, however, expected. Children are going to make mistakes over and over again, but they need the guidance of competent adults to guide them along the way. I watched my father very closely while I was growing up. What I remember learning the most was the duties and responsibilities of a man that go with taking care and providing for his family. I don't ever recall one day when I was wondering whether or not Daddy was coming home.

For as long as I could remember, Daddy held down a steady job. My father did not bounce around from job to job because he knew that this would be a sign of instability. This type of man was not the exception in my neighborhood.

He was the norm. This is what I recall men doing for their families in the late 1970s and early 1980s. Where has this type of man gone? I know they are still out there.

There was a time, if a child was caught misbehaving in public, whatever adult from the neighborhood caught him/her misbehaving they would deal with him/her right then and there. Believe me when I tell you that it did not stop there. Many times these adults would take you home to your parents and tell them not only what you did but the punishment they put on you in the streets. In my neighborhood, it was safer to get punished by your neighbors than your parents. My father had a way of making punishment for his children last weeks at a time. Some people today may say that this was cruel. I say, twenty-five years later, that this was parenting.

Members of the community did not turn their backs to the foolishness that was taking place in their neighborhoods. There was a time when neighbors in communities did not wait until a crime was committed before they called the police. If they thought a crime was about to be committed they were on the phone with 9-1-1, giving a description of the perpetrators. I don't think that was harsh at all. I think it was proactive of people who lived in communities who wanted to maintain a vibrant, safe, and clean community.

The following is a story about two young boys who grew up in the same neighborhood with access to similar resources but yet chose different paths in life.

Story 1

A friend of mine grew up in the same neighborhood as I. He came from a two-income family household. His father was a hard worker, working in the auto industry. His mother was also a hard worker and she worked in retail/sales. They both had one common goal as parents. They both wanted to see their son grow up to be a productive member of society. Anything short of that, in their minds, they felt would be unacceptable. This was not a goal his parents established after my friend reached thirteen or fourteen years old. This was a goal that was established when my friend was still in diapers.

Hard work and determination was ingrained in my friend at an early age. Shoveling snow in the winter time to cutting grass in the summer, at eight years old my friend had more experience working outside than a thirty-year-old construction worker. At the age of nine, my friend had a paper route where he delivered the local paper to the community every morning and three evenings during the week. This taught him the responsibility of waking himself up every morning and committing himself to a task. This was a task which paid him every two weeks. So at a very young age, he learned the concept of earning a paycheck. He did this job for two years, earning approximately $35 per week. To some that might not sound like a lot of money. But to a nine-year-old kid who loved to play video games and occasionally buy a few items for himself in 1984, this was a gold mine.

My friend worked hard every day, just as he had seen his father work. His father had grown up in a time when you either worked or went to school. There was no time for both. His father's goal was to teach his son several things at once. Stability, responsibility, hard work, dedication, reliability, and trustworthiness, to name a few, were the things his father wanted him to have, in addition to him furthering his education. My friend never complained or groaned about working. If he could have worked more, he would have. However, his parents wanted him to strike a balance between education and working. He worked because that was what he was taught to do.

My friend had never seen his father strike his mother. The only time he saw his father put his hands on his mother was in a loving way. His father did not rule over his mother with his fist. His father truly believed in leadership and believed in the concept of leading by example. His father believed that men were put on this earth to lead their families, not destroy them. The father told his son that when a family is in disarray and the family is being led by the father, God ultimately holds the father responsible. It is for this reason his father said, "You cannot take fatherhood and manhood lightly." This is how the Bible speaks of men.

His father taught his son that he had a duty and a responsibility to provide for his family and do what was right. By the time my friend was eleven years old, he had saved up $400 that he made from delivering newspapers. He mastered the art of discipline. My friend's father taught him about money and bank accounts. The young boy opened his first savings account at eleven years old. He would go to the bank to make a deposit, and all the tellers knew him and his parents by first name. One teller made mention that he was the only eleven-year-old in town making deposits to his saving account every week.

The young boy watched his father come home every week and give his paycheck to his mother. He asked his father one day, "Dad, why do you give Momma your whole paycheck?" His father replied, "Son, what your mother gives me in return will outweigh any amount of money I bring home. She takes care of the family, makes sure I have what I need to be able to work, and she is a better manager of money than I am."

From the ages eleven to seventeen, my friend worked odd jobs there in the neighborhood to earn extra money. His father emphasized to him that education was the key to working smarter instead of working harder. My friend stayed busy most of the time. He really did not have much time to even think about getting into trouble. His father was not a lazy man by any stretch of the imagination. He never allowed his son to be lazy, and this proved to pay off huge dividends in later years. He stayed preoccupied doing other things, which was all part of his father's master plan. His father was aware of the dangers that were out there in the streets. His father knew that there were not many options for a young black kid, who had a record, in Chicago. So to give his son a fighting chance, his father did what he could to ensure his son stayed away from trouble.

My friend's parents were his first role models. This is what his parents wanted. His role models did not come from the streets or the television set. His role models were not professional athletes or celebrities. His father was there to teach him the things that needed to be done in order for him to have a productive life. His mother was there to provide a balance. The young boy aspired to be half the man, father, and husband his father was to him and his family while he was growing up. Even though his father did not get very far in school, his father was nevertheless his source of inspiration.

As he got a little older, my friend's father placed more responsibility on him. His father emphasized, "No matter how much you achieve or don't achieve in life, you are still held accountable to somebody." His father kept a tight hold on him. If his son was out after it had gotten dark, his father knew his whereabouts. This is something that is no longer common practice in today's society. "An idle mind is the devil's workshop" was one of his parents favorite quotes.

Story 2

My other friend whom I grew up with also came from a two-income household, where his mother and father worked. His mother worked as a hair stylist at the local hair salon five days a week and made a modest living. His father, on the other hand, was the neighborhood drug dealer.

My friend was a fast learner, and this applied to everything he did. This guy was never forced to do anything by his parents. There was no responsibility, there was no dedication, and there was no commitment to a worthy cause or any of that. My friend never saw his father gainfully employed, and as a result he did not place much emphasis on the working-class people. His father was known as the neighborhood hustler. In the streets of America, much is to be said about a young man who wants to grow up and be a hustler. A hustler, according to his father's definition, was anybody who is a master at getting over on everybody. A hustler was the man who knew how to get all he could with the least amount of effort possible. This was his teaching model. His father's theory was "easy come easy go." This is how he felt about his money and his women. This is the model by which he instructed his son to follow.

I said my friend's mother was a hair stylist by day, but what I did not say was that at night she was the neighborhood crackhead. It must be really tough growing up in a neighborhood and everybody knowing that your mom does drugs. The psychological impact of this alone is mind-boggling. Pimping women, selling dope, working odd jobs, and going from pillar to post only gets you so far. When my friend was twelve years old, his father was eventually arrested on felony, drugs, and robbery charges. Over the next twenty years, his father was in and out of jail for the same old thing.

His father never taught him what he needed to know to be a productive man. The streets became his father, the streets showed him love, and it was the streets that he respected. I have never met anyone in the streets that was worth going to jail for or putting my life on the line. Men who live on the streets are masters at corrupting the minds of young boys and girls and getting them to do whatever they ask them to do. If you are not being a father to your child, the drug dealers, gang bangers, and the street pimps will. Remember that if nothing else.

The young boy did not make terrible grades. There was however, room for improvement. I remember teachers from the school would call my friend's house crying out to his parents to have a conference to see if there was anything else that could be done to ensure the academic success of my friend. His parents never made any of the conferences, never attended any of the PTA meetings, never promoted education, and for all intents and purposes were absentee parents. As a result, my friend dropped out of school at sixteen. He fell by the wayside and was on his way to becoming another statistic.

My friend had an older brother named Charles. Charles was four years older than his younger brother. Charles was just like his father. You have to remember, the apple never falls too far away from the tree. His father had a distinguished career in the field of being a criminal. The savvy style of being a criminal rubbed off on both of his sons. When Charles was seventeen years old, he was driving around town in a gold Cadillac. The Cadillac was the most luxurious car driven at the time. Today, the Cadillac has been overtaken by Mercedes Benz, Audi, Lincoln, and Lexus, to name a few. The Caddy was the car back in the day. Charles pulled up to an intersection, and he saw his younger brother walking. Younger brothers tend to adore their older brothers. My friend ran up to the car and told his big brother how much he loved his new car. The Cadillac was gold with twenty-inch-chrome wheels. The vehicle drew lots of attention as it was being driven down the street. My friend asked his brother "Where did you get the car?" His brother replied, "It's a loaner." His brother was actually telling the truth in regard to the vehicle being a loaner. But there were several problems. First, his brother was not twenty-one years old; therefore, he was not old enough to rent a car. Second, his brother did not have a driver's license. Third, the car did not belong to his brother and was used in the commission of several felony offenses from neighboring cities. The vehicle his brother was driving was also reported stolen from a neighboring city, just east of where my friend lived.

It seemed that my friend made one bad decision after another. He got into the car with his brother and they began to drive around. His brother began reaching speeds of ten to fifteen miles above the posted speed limit. He was going about fifty miles per hour in a thirty-five, when he passed a patrol officer who recognized the license plates on the Cadillac. The license plates on the Cadillac was on the patrol officer's hot sheet. A hot sheet is a list of stolen cars printed out for police officers as a quick reference prior to them beginning to start their shift. The officer passed the Cadillac and immediately did a U-turn. The officer pulled closer to the rear of the Cadillac and conducted a license plate check over the radio to get confirmation that the vehicle had been reported stolen. This is standard practice for most law enforcement agencies prior to performing felony stops on reported stolen vehicles.

The vehicle was confirmed stolen and by this time, the patrol officer had several more patrol units with him. They activated their emergency lights on the Cadillac. Both boys began to get into a panic mode and drove approximately one mile before they decided to pull over. Once the vehicle was pulled over, several officers ran up to the vehicle with guns drawn, yelling and screaming loud verbal commands. "Don't move, let me see your hands," one officer yelled. "Get out the car now," another officer yelled. Both boys, frightened and confused, just froze in one spot. Finally, both boys, scared out of their minds, complied with the verbal directives of the officers. The police officers, not knowing who or what was inside the vehicle, approached the vehicle tactfully and safely. Both boys were handcuffed and taken into custody.

The seventeen-year-old was arrested and charged with Grand Theft Auto. He already had prior records for misdemeanor charges in the past. My friend, who was twelve years old, was just one month away from his thirteenth birthday. He was also arrested, but was field released to his parents at police headquarters. Because of his age, he was not charged with anything. Little did I know, this would be the first of many involvements with local law enforcement and my friend for the next twenty years.

By the time my friend was seventeen years old, he had been arrested seven times for theft, criminal mischief, and burglary. He was on the career track of his father. He told me one day that it was society's fault that he turned out the way that he did. He blamed his parents for not doing more. He blamed his friends for not stepping up and pulling him in the right direction. His complaints may have some merit. The one person that I did not hear him blame was himself. He took absolutely no responsibility for the decisions he made. The one-hundred-thousand-dollar question is, does he have a point? Are all of us that were the closest to him to blame? Could I have done more? Could we have done more? Even though we were children at the time, could I have used more of my influence on him to encourage him to do other things? These are questions that I'm not sure can be answered.

When I think about the twenty-first century man and the legacy we are leaving behind for our children, I am concerned. I really question the footsteps we are expecting our children to follow. Senator Hillary Clinton once said, "It takes a village to raise a child." I believe this wholeheartedly. I am particularly concerned about this issue in the black community. Black people are and always will be a powerful economic force in the United States. Truth be told, this great country we live in today was built from the blood, tears, and sweat on the backs of black people. This is not to say that other groups did not contribute to this country's building and advancement. Indeed they have. It is just noted that black people were brought to this country against their will and exploited for over two hundred years, bringing this country to what it is today.

I am afraid that if we don't take the time to learn about our history, so that we can teach our history to the next generation, then we are destined to repeat it. With this said, there are many aspects of U.S. history that I don't ever want to be repeated. In order for this to happen, we need to get back to the basics. We need to get back to being the hard workers that we were once applauded for. We need to get back to placing premiums on our families and their development. We need to get back to being the backbones of our family that we once were. It is for these reasons and many others why you have no other choice, and you need to stand up and figure out the importance of *Why You Need to Be the Man*.

Chapter 1

Back In The Day

As I was growing up, my parents made sure that even though we did not have everything that we wanted, we definitely had everything we needed. We never lacked anything. I grew up with two older sisters, Jacquelyn and Joyce, and a younger brother, Shannon. Each one of us developed our own individual talents and we are all self-sufficient adults today. This could not have been possible without the assistance of people like Grandma Olivee, Grandpa Willie Ward, our parents, and a host of others I don't have room to name. The goal of both of our parents was to ensure that all of their children were self-sufficient and productive individuals. They did a fine job and may God bless their souls.

As a child, you don't really concern yourself with the day-to-day responsibilities of what is required to live. I was not concerned with how much light, gas, or water I used. I was not concerned with what my parents wanted to do. My only concern was what I wanted to do. I was not concerned about paying a mortgage, paying health insurance, putting gas in the car, etc. This was adult stuff. It did not apply to me. At least that is what I thought. When I started to hit those teen years, my parents started painting a much clearer picture to me of what it took to live. But living was not good enough. I needed to be trained on how to live responsibly. When responsibility kicked in, my feet hit the ground running. Accountability was a new word that was added to my vocabulary at the age of twelve. Things started to become a little different as I was beginning to go through a transitional stage at that time of my life. I did not know it yet, but the foundation by which to prepare me for manhood had already been laid out. My father laid it when I was too young to even remember.

My mother, like most mothers, was the more nurturing parent. She did things for me and the other children that she had no business doing. A lot of things my mother did, my dad never had any knowledge of. This was a tool my mother used to keep us all in line, especially me. When I would ask my mother a question, and she did not really want to answer it, she would say go ask your father. Often times, I knew the answer to my question before I would even ask him. My eldest sister, Joyce, who is ten years my senior would always tease me by saying things like, "You are Momma's favorite and you can do no wrong in her eyes." I would then come back and say, "So what, I have Momma and you have Daddy, so what is the difference?" It was really nice growing up with siblings. This is especially the case when you have the type of siblings that you idolize and want to be like. This was a fortunate situation to grow up in, and I will always cherish those family memories.

I watched my eldest sister, Joyce, go through the rigors of college. When Joyce started college, I was only eight years old. I remember when she invited me to the campus of Northern Illinois University during her first year of college. NIU was only ninety miles from Chicago. I spent the entire weekend with my sister on a college campus. I watched how much fun the students were having. I saw all the studying and hard work that the students were putting into their studies. While I was there during that weekend, I received a lot of attention. I loved every minute of it too. My sister's friends would come to her dorm room, and I was known as Joyce's cute little brother. My sister even let me hang out with her and some of her friends in the student lounge area. I was in awe at what I was exposed to at eight years old. During this weekend stay, I felt like I was a college student. I felt like the little man on the big campus. This was a major milestone in my little life at that time.

I realized at that very moment that one day I would have my day, going to college. I watched my sister, but she did not know at that time the impact that spending one weekend with her away at school had on me. This provided the inspiration that I needed that I eventually would act on. I am sure my sister has done a lot of things for me over the years, especially when I was not able to do them myself. But, the one thing that stands out was when she took the time out of her schedule to spend the weekend with her little brother away at college.

In the 1980s, Bill Cosby had a hit TV show, *The Cosby Show*, which ran for eight seasons. *The Cosby Show* was a depiction of an African American family that put a premium on family values, internal strength, and higher education. Each show had a positive story line and a life lesson. Bill Cosby, who acted as Cliff Huxtable, and Phylicia Rashad, who played his wife, Clair Huxtable, were black professionals living in New York. *The Cosby Show* was the first TV sitcom that showed America that black families also aspire to have the American dream. A doctor for a father and a lawyer for a mother were inspirational for young black couples as well as young black children who could achieve the same desired success. Bill Cosby was another source who motivated me to further my education and to earn my place in the world.

My father kept everything in perspective. My dad grew up in the southern part of the United States. He was born in Tennessee and later moved to Hayti, Missouri. It was in Missouri where my parents actually met. My mother's name was Joyce Marie Ward. My parents were high-school sweethearts in the 1950s. In the summer of 1956, they got married and packed up and moved to Chicago, Illinois. It was in Chicago where my parents made a life for themselves and raised their children. They spent forty-two years together until my mother left her earthly life on March 23, 1998.

My father's name was Samuel Lee Digby Sr. He departed his earthly life 10 years after my mother on November 23, 2008. He was one of the hardest working men I have ever known. Laziness was never an issue in the Digby household. Of all the words I could use to describe my father, laziness would not be one of them. My father was one of those guys who seemed to always make the best out of a terrible situation. He assumed that role with his younger siblings after his parents died and continued to assume that role after he had children of his own.

I benefited greatly by having a strong male presence in my life. I had the opportunity to watch not only my father, but also the other men my dad hung around with, who were also positive influences on me. Everywhere my dad went I wanted to go. I think after children get to a certain age, they begin to identify with the same-sex parent. I loved my mom dearly, but after I became eleven years old, I wanted to learn "man stuff." This is my advice to all the men and women who are reading this book. Hear me, when I say, "It takes a man to teach a boy how to be a man." I cannot overemphasize that. This is not to say that boys cannot learn from women. Indeed this is not the case. Some of my greatest teachings in life were taught to me by women. But, we need to understand, a woman can never know what it truly feels like to walk in the shoes of a man. With this said, why do many men allow women to continue to fight an uphill battle of trying to raise boys on their own. Guys, you need to get involved and make your presence felt.

I got a chance to learn bits and parts of what it takes to be a man from several of my dad's friends and my uncles. My father spent quite a bit of time around my uncle, Rev. Stratton Knight. Uncle Stratton was like a walking encyclopedia. There was never a dull moment went he was in the room. I received a lot of spiritual support from Uncle Stratton over the years. My Uncle Stratton has been in the ministry longer than I have been on this earth. He always reminded me to keep God first in all that I do. If I did that, I couldn't possibly go wrong. I remember when I turned sixteen and got my driver's license and my first car, the first place I wanted to drive was my Uncle Stratton's house. I wanted to show him that I had a driver's license and that I could hit the road just like him. I often wonder how my life would have been different if I had not been exposed to strong men. My uncle and my father were the epitomes of what a strong man is supposed to do. Sometimes I think about the young boys who grow up without the presence of any strong man by which to learn from. This would be a tough situation to be in. I was truly blessed.

My father worked for Ford Motor Company for thirty years. He worked on the assembly line, producing what he thought was one of America's finest automobiles. My father took pride in hard work, and he was very dedicated in all he did. I saw my father get up every morning at 4:00 a.m. to get ready for his morning shift at the assembly plant. My father did not have to be at work until

6:00 a.m., and we only lived ten minutes from his job. My father's philosophy was that it was better to be one hour early than five minutes late. Realistically, my father worked only eight hours a day, but he spent nine and a half hours at his job, because he liked to be early. My father was not the type of man to take on a job and complete only half of it.

My father was not the type of man to borrow money from people and not repay his debts. He was just the opposite. He encouraged me at an early age to make sure that I position myself financially to where I would never have to borrow money from anyone. I remember asking my father why I shouldn't borrow money from people, because everyone else was doing it. My father advised me that just because everyone else is doing something that does not mean that it is OK. I researched it a little further and found out what the Bible says about borrowing money. Proverbs 22:7 says, *the rich ruleth over the poor, and the borrower is the servant to the lender.*

My father took pride in doing a job that benefited society. When my father started working for Ford Motor Company in 1964, 40 percent of the vehicles that were on the roadways at the time were Ford products. My dad drove a Ford car for as long as I could remember. His philosophy was to keep the American autoworkers working, at all costs. Not only did my father drive a Ford, but everyone in my family owned a Ford vehicle as well. I also had several other family members that worked for Ford. There was even a period of time when Dad did not want any cars parked in the driveway that were not made by Ford. Ford fed our family while I was growing up. My father worked for Ford Motor Company for thirty years and this company even provided me with some tuition assistance for college. The only requirements were that I pick a school that I wanted to attend and I was a dependent of a Ford Motor Company employee. This was all they needed to verify and they cut a check. I have the same deep, burning passion for Ford cars that my dad had. It is for this reason and many others that I have always bought a Ford and will continue to buy Ford products the rest of my days.

My father was an educated man. He was not educated in the sense of what society says a man needs to be educated. You see my father never finished high school. He had to drop out of high school to help support his family. My father obtained his knowledge from learning the world around him. The education he received could not be taught in a book. The education he passed down to his children could not be taught in a classroom. Things were not as easy to come by in the 1980s, as they are now. Today information is at your fingertips with the click of a button. In the 1980s, if I wanted information on something, I had to physically go and get it, or send for it by mail, which sometimes took a week or longer. I remember my mother saying to me that sometimes the best type of sense is "bought sense." Since I have now been on this earth thirty plus years, I have come to realize that common sense is not all that common.

My father's favorite newspaper while I was growing up was the *Chicago Sun-Times*. This newspaper sprouted up several debates between my dad and I over the dinner table. When my father and I would disagree about an issue in the paper, my dad would just end the disagreement and tell me to just figure it out on my own. Those were the good old days. Gone are the days when families would sit together in the evening time and have dinner as a family unit. Gone are the days when there were no more than two television sets in the house. As I think back, everyone in my household knew what the other people in the household were doing because there was no Internet, PlayStation, MySpace, or Facebook. There were not as many external distractions that came between the families as there are today. My father was the type of person who knew everything about everything. At least that is what we thought as children. Even if my dad could not answer a question and someone else in the room could, he would still graciously take the credit just for being in the presence when the question was answered. Our family got plenty of good laughs as a result of Dad's tactics.

My grandfather, Willie Ward, had an interesting theory about raising children. Before he passed away in October 1999, he would always say, "Parents are no longer raising their children. They are just feeding them and watching them grow." When my grandfather passed away, he was ninety-four years old. He too had seen and done a lot of good for his community during his time on earth. He had seen some historical events in his lifetime. He had witnessed the first man land on the moon. He lived through some of this country's darkest time periods. He lived through the Great Depression. He lived through World

War I, World War II, the Korean War, and Vietnam. He lived through the dark ages of segregation and Jim Crow. He lived through the Civil Rights Movement. He had seen the struggles that black men faced during times of adversity in the United States. The beauty of all this was that he lived long enough to share his knowledge and wisdom with me and other young people. Prior to passing away, my grandfather was concerned about the direction this country was going in. He was unhappy with the black race as a whole. His position was that even though black people had made strides and continued to progress, there were still some areas in which black people were severely deficient.

He was concerned that the perception of the black man was that of "lazy." He told me that this really bothered him because he came from a time period where the black man was known for his hard work and dedication. He was concerned that the black male, compared to his white counterpart, was not raising his children like he once was during the pre-civil-rights era. He felt that with all the progress that black people were making, the one thing that held black people together since the post-slavery era was family, and the family unit was deteriorating in the black community. During the 1980's and 1990's, there was an overwhelming desire to get strung out on crack. This epidemic hit all races in the United States hard, especially the black community. The knowledge and wisdom my grandfather shared was priceless.

My grandmother, Olivee Smith, kept me grounded in the church. She made sure that I knew God and that I would be held accountable to Him for any wrongdoing. I remember going to several different churches on the west side of Chicago, with my grandmother giving holiday speeches. My mother and grandmother would get together and write speeches for me to say during Thanksgiving, Christmas, and Easter programs. They wrote speeches for me for years, and every year I would be added to a church children's program to deliver my speech. I remember during the school year I had homework to do from school. After I completed my homework, I was required to stay up an extra hour, memorizing the speeches my mom and her mother wrote for me. I memorized every speech and was asked by several churches to come back again to be a part of future children's programs. This was a terrific honor and one of my proudest accomplishments while growing up.

My grandmother and mother had no idea what they were preparing me for when I was giving speeches in front of church congregations as a child at ten and eleven years old. This taught me not to be afraid of speaking before large groups of people. I learned at a young age to be calm and say what was on my heart. I developed eye contact with my audience. I always felt a connection when I was speaking to them. This was an amazing feeling especially after I completed my speech. My mother and grandmother had a terrific skill in writing speeches even though they had not spent one day in a college classroom. My mother did graduate from high school, but my grandmother never finished. The words they used in my speeches were words I had no idea existed in their vocabulary. I was still young at the time, but as time went by, I began to realize what an honor, privilege, and blessing it was to have both of these women around. These women contributed significantly to my development as a Christian and as a man.

A mother's love for her children is unconditional. A true mother's love is unlike anything else that you can experience. Nobody will do for you what your mother will do. If you who have a mother that is still around, honor her every chance you get. Tell your mother thank-you for putting up with your mess over the years. Believe me when I tell you this is the only payment you can give her. For those women who have had to raise boys as a single parent, I commend you especially if your boys beat the odds. If you are one of those men who were raised by a single mother and did not have a relationship with your father think about how you felt without your dad, if you are contemplating on leaving your wife and children. I want you to think about how you felt when you had questions about manhood that your mother had to answer, because Dad was not around. Therefore, I cherish the memories my mother made with me. She was indeed my inspiration, and I know my life would have been considerably different without her.

A developing child's mind is like a bank account. If you don't make any deposits, you cannot expect to make any withdrawals. Proverbs 22:6 says, *train up a child in the way he should go, and when they get old they shall not depart from it*. What does this really mean? I'm here to tell you that it does not mean that children will not make mistakes or stray from the parents' teachings. It means that as adults we have a moral responsibility to teach and train our children on the right and wrong things to do. As parents, if we do this, when our children become adults and begin to experience life's complexities, when they go through the decision-making process they will recall the teachings from Momma and Daddy. It is imperative that we all use every moment we have with our children as teaching moments. Our youths are in dire need of guidance and direction and only the older generations can help the younger generation succeed.

When I was about eleven years old, the one thing I feared more than anything else was death. I'm not talking about the death of myself. I feared the death of one or both of my parents, while I was still a child. I often remember asking myself questions such as, what would I do if one of my parents died while I was growing up? What would happen to the rest of the family unit? How would I survive? All of these questions raced through my mind. I knew several children I went to school with who had lost a parent while growing up and the stories they told were horrific. I heard stories about the mean stepfather or mean stepmother. I heard stories of the beatings from Momma's new boyfriend. I did, however, find comfort in God who answered my prayer. The following is a childhood prayer I used to say.

The Prayer

"God, Thank You for another day. Thank You for waking me up this morning and keeping me safe at night. God, please watch over my parents. Please let them stay around long enough to watch me become an adult. Lord, I do not want to stay with relatives or have a stepparent come into my life to help raise me. Lord, teach me what I need to know so that one day, I can be a good man. God, I know the day will come when You will take my parents away with You but I just ask that You allow me to be able to take care of myself. Momma has warned me that none of us know the day, nor, the hour when You will call us home, but God, please make sure that I am in a position to deal with it. God, I know that I have not always done good and sometimes I did not listen to my parents when I was supposed to, but their teachings are right and I know that You are right. God, hear my prayer in Jesus's name, I pray, Amen!"

My grandmother taught me how to humble myself and pray. In today's society, do we even have grandmothers like her anymore? My mother always told me, "Jr., get you something that nobody can ever take away from you. An education." I did not quite understand that at first, but as time went on it became increasingly clear what Momma was talking about. My mother did not go any further than high school, but she was determined that her children would go to college. In later years, I realized that the bank could take your house if you don't pay the mortgage, the bank could take your car if you don't pay the car note, and your boss could fire you from your position if you fail to perform or in some cases if they don't like you. Momma's theory proved true. I finally understood what she was talking about. Once you arm yourself with an education, there is nothing anybody can do to take that away from you. Once you have been trained for a particular skill, that skill is yours forever and the only thing you have to do at that point is stay up to date with the latest changes and trends. There will always be people in the world who will try to discredit you and talk bad about you; however, it does not matter. What matters is that you are standing on the shoulders of those who stood before you. Education is a prize that was bought and paid for with the blood and sweat of our ancestors. Those of you who get any education, that education does not just belong to you. It belongs to those who also sacrificed life as they knew it in order for you to get that education. That education belongs to future generations who, it is hopeful, one day will benefit from your knowledge. If you fail to acknowledge this then you are doing yourself a great disservice.

Chapter 2

Don't Talk About It; Be About It

My family and I enjoyed life's little pleasures. I don't want to imply that I never had any fun. Indeed that was not the case. My parents realized early during their child-rearing years that they were not raising children. They were raising adults because a fully functioning adult is the final product. Years ago, neighborhoods took care of each other. We were all our brothers' keepers. What has happened to that sentiment? If the government is not going to acknowledge the problems we are having with our youths, then parents have an obligation to handle it on their own. In no way do I want to pretend that I have it altogether and have not made mistakes. Believe me, this is not the case. I am a work in progress, just like the next person. I have made mistakes. Truth be told, I have many more mistakes to make before I leave this earth.

It is because of God's grace, and His grace alone, that we have made it this far. Too often many people get so caught up with doing their own thing that they forget to give credit where credit is due. Whenever I hear people tell me they have experience in something, I always say to myself that experience is another name for mistakes. If you do something wrong for a long time, you should figure out where you are going wrong at some point and get it right. God has given each one of us a precious gift called a mind. It is up to you to figure out how and what purpose God has for your mind.

I do believe that the life we live is a direct result of the decisions we make. The same holds true for our children. Pastor Rick Warren wrote a book in 2002, titled, *The Purpose Driven Life*. Pastor Warren takes you on a forty-day journey in his book to assist his readers with finding out just why God put you here on earth. Pastor Warren's emphasis is that none of us are an accident and God has a master plan that He wants to execute. The only question is will we allow Him to? To anyone who is interested in finding themselves and understanding that they have a purpose here on earth, I recommend reading Warren's book; it will be a life-changing experience.

Men, you need to get off that couch, put that beer down, and stop bowling with the boys on the weekend, so you can begin taking control of your household and becoming more involved in your children's extracurricular activities. If you can't find an opportunity to help with the crisis our young people are facing, don't just throw your hands up in the air and say oh well. Go and create an opportunity yourself. Figure out what you can do to benefit mankind. Remember that thing that God gave you? A mind. Please put it to good use. Things such as launching a mentoring campaign in your community can be a great starting point. If you are a member of a church, find out what programs the church currently has going on for the youths and get involved. I drive through poverty-stricken neighborhoods all the time, and it never seems to amaze me that the lights in the churches are always turned off during the evenings and at night. This is the time the lights need to be turned on. It is during the night-time hours that we are losing our youths to the streets. This is particularly the case in minority neighborhoods. Let's get it together men and give back to our communities. They need us.

I try to do whatever I can to assist organizations and churches that assist young people in the community on how to dress for success. I don't believe that the only day you should dress conservatively is on Sunday. I stress to the younger generation that if they want to be successful in the workforce, they must dress for the job they want, not the one they have. I have seen young men come to job interviews with sagging pants, expecting someone who is dressed in business attire to give them a shot. Whatever expectation you may have had in gaining employment is thrown out the window if you show up looking like you just crawled out of the bed. Young men, *pull up your pants*. This is not cute or attractive. It is embarrassing and disgraceful. Have a little more respect for yourself than this. I'm speaking to the young men as a brother, a father, a mentor, or whatever else I need to be. Sometimes your physical appearance is all a person sees before they talk to you. You will never get a second chance to make a first impression. Young men, you want your first impression to be a lasting one, especially if somebody has something that you want or need. Men, it is our job to guide these young brothers in the right direction. They are all a reflection of us.

I have seen young ladies come to job interviews and I would ask them, are you applying for a job or are you on your way to the nightclub? Some of the responses I got you would not believe. I have met young men in the community who have told me that they want to be better and do better. The only problem is that they don't know how or where to start. This is where mentoring or being a role model comes into play.

I remember in 2003, I was working an off-duty job at a church. Working off duty is something that most police officers do to earn extra money. I must admit, it can also be a very powerful networking tool if used properly. While working at this church, I had a fourteen-year-old boy approach me. The young man asked me a question I was too proud to answer. He asked me, "Can you teach me how to tie a tie?" I stopped and paused for a moment to internalize what this young man was asking me. Here stood a boy whom I had never seen before and he had asked me to teach him how to do something. Notice the language. The young man did not ask me to do something for him. He asked me to teach him to do something on his own. This young man struck me as being very articulate for his age. He was not the typical fourteen-year-old kid in the streets. As I looked at this young man, he had a glow about himself that said, "success." There is an old saying, "if I cook you a meal, then I feed you for a day, but if I teach how to cook a meal then I feed you for lifetime." I was honored to show this young man how to tie a tie. The funny part about it is that I only had to show the young man how to tie a tie one time. Every Sunday, from that point forward when I would see this young man, he had on a tie. There is so much we can do for our youths that does not cost any money.

Once you have programs started and see their effectiveness, you will be in a much better position to ask for government funding for a particular project or program that has demonstrated its effectiveness for the community. Though nothing is guaranteed, government agencies are more likely to support programs that are already established than those that appear to have not gotten off the ground. Establish informal as well as formal relationships with your local elected officials. The problems that we see in our inner cities, as far as I'm concerned, are all local issues. They are not Washington's problems. When you start getting things done on the local level and your elected officials know that you are a force to be reckoned with, you will set a great platform for national exposure. By conducting your business in this fashion, your elected officials will begin to hear your concerns and become more responsive. Until politicians become responsive to the needs of the communities they serve, everything they say is nothing more then political rhetoric.

As local elected officials become more responsive, it is more likely that your agenda will appear on the front steps of Capitol Hill. Your issues will never end up on the steps of Capitol Hill as long as you keep sitting in front of the television set, hoping that the great messiah is going to come bursting through the TV screen with the right answers. I'm sorry to be a disappointment, but it does not work that way. Please keep in mind that every politician in Washington, DC, represents a local government from somewhere in the United States. I am really concerned that many of our youths have lost their drive to find out what their purpose is on this earth. Some of our children are no longer living a life. They merely exist from day to day without any kind of hope or vision.

In terms of education, economic prosperity, financial stability, and community growth, will this next generation of American children acquire the same or even more than their parents have acquired? I am particularly concerned with our inner city Black and Latino youths. Why is there such a large degree of hopelessness brewing in the minds of our young people today? We can either take care of the problem now to turn this crisis around, or, the problem will take care of us in the future. In twenty years, who do you think will be working at the health care facilities? Who do you think will be our future doctors, lawyers, teachers, and politicians? Who do you think will be our robbers, homeless people, killers, and drug dealers? The answer is real simple. These individuals will all come from the same generation of children. The children of today will become the leaders of tomorrow, with proper guidance and instruction. Or, the children of today will become the inmates and criminals of tomorrow, bearing a burden on the taxpayers' dollar. If we fail to prepare our children for the future, this will be the beginning of the end of the world as we know it. Success is nothing more than preparation and opportunity meeting up together. To have one without the other would mean that anything accomplished would be short-lived.

As many of you are aware, the year 2009, brought about some massive changes to the United States unlike this country has ever seen. The United States has been rocked with the highest unemployment rate since the 1930s, holding just under 10 percent. There is a huge battle going on in our Congress in overhauling our current health care system which would have a tremendous impact on millions of Americans who currently don't have access to health care. Budget constraints have all but crippled local and state governments resulting in massive layoffs, furlough days for government employees, and social programs being cut and in some cases being eliminated altogether. All of us have friends or relatives who have lost their homes along with their ability to feed and take care of their families. All of us have friends or relatives whose retirement accounts and emergency savings accounts have been cut in half and in some cases wiped out completely. With everything that is going on in our country, we must still find a way to keep the faith. This is not the time to self-destruct. Dr. Martin Luther King Jr., one of the greatest civil rights leaders of the twentieth century, said, "You cannot measure a man's character during times of prosperity; the true measurement of a man's character is during times of adversity." No matter how bad you think you may have it, remember there is somebody somewhere in this world that has it a lot worse than you, and they are still making it through the storm. Philippians 4:19 says, "But my God, shall supply all your need according to his riches in glory by Jesus Christ." In God's word, He did not say that He would supply some of our needs. He said that He would supply all of our needs. As long as He supplies all of our needs, we will never be without.

Teaching the Youngsters

I have been a law enforcement officer for ten years. Prior to becoming a police officer, I remember I would often ask myself, what could I do to have an impact on future generations? My goal was to establish a long legacy by which future generations could follow. This is what I think leaders like Dr. Martin Luther King Jr., Rosa Parks, Dr. W. E. B. DuBois, and Booker T. Washington set out to do. They wanted to leave the world in a better place than it was when they arrived. This is indeed what I intend to do. I want to contribute to the knowledge base so that a hundred years from now, a thriving young person can hear or read my words and take it to the next level, during their lifetime.

I believe as men we need to put a premium on helping our families become the best that they can be. We also need to help our fellow brothers and sisters achieve the same. What is success if you can't help bring out the best in other people? I believe that once you leave this earthly life and you transition into your eternal life, God is not going to be overly concerned with what you did for yourself. God is not going to ask you how many degrees you earned on earth. God is not going to be concerned with how much money you have in your 401(k) or other retirement accounts. God is going to look over your life and mine and ask, what have you done for my people? On Judgment Day when you are asked that question, how do you think you will respond? I tell you this, when it's my time, I want to no doubt show that I have done all I could for mankind and to make this a better world for all of us.

The Law Enforcement Teacher

It is my belief that the quickest way for anyone to find peace and be successful is to develop success through other people. God is going to want to know how the life that He blessed you with been used to impact the lives of His children. Think about that for a minute. Once I got into law enforcement, I found that I had a passion for teaching. I thought about doing substitute teaching as a part-time job with the local school district; however, my full-time job schedule would not allow me to do that. Then I found the ultimate opportunity that existed right under my nose. I immediately began teaching in the Dallas Independent School District as an LETS officer.

LETS is an acronym for law enforcement teaching students. LETS is a cooperative program between the Dallas Police Department and the Dallas Independent School District where police officers go into the elementary schools to teach classes on character education. LETS is a proactive program geared toward prevention of adverse behavior in our youths before it starts. Prevention programs are less expensive than intervention programs. When you are dealing with intervention programs, adverse behavior has already begun. It means considerably more money, time, and resources has to be put into this type of program than in prevention programs. An example of intervention programs would be those that exist in the penal institutions or the penal institution itself.

I was blessed with the opportunity to go inside the classrooms of fourth, fifth, and sixth grade students in Dallas and teach them the importance of building and maintaining good character. More importantly, I wanted the students in the inner city to see the police in a different light. I wanted them to understand that I was a person just like them and cared about them as if I were their parent. I was not some alien from a far away land who didn't have a clue about reality or what was going on. I was surprised to find out that many of the students I taught in class initially thought that all I did was ride around in my squad car everyday, putting people in jail and being this big bad tough guy. They thought that I never slept, never did anything with my family, spent nights at the jailhouse, and a host of other ideas that were way out there. The goal for me at the very beginning of teaching every class was to let my students know that first of all, I was approachable. I wanted them to feel comfortable with me and let them know that I was there to help and not hinder. If I were unsuccessful at establishing this rapport at the beginning, there was no way the students would have believed a word I said or trusted me. Secondly, I wanted to let them know that I was expecting to learn just as much from them as they would from me. They were surprised when I said I wanted to learn from them. Their little young minds could not fathom the idea that a policeman was in their class, expecting to learn something from them. This made them feel worthy and respected. Third, I needed my students to know that there was no difference between them and me. I told them that I was probably the age of a lot of their parents, and I was going to talk to them as such.

Young people need to know that you value their opinion. This does not mean that you give in to them. It just means that you are respecting their thinking process, and you are acknowledging their right to be heard. I do feel that I learned a great deal from these kids. Every class I taught was different, and I enjoyed them all. What I learned during the eight years I have taught LETS is that some of these students are just begging for hope. They want somebody to believe in them and their ability to succeed. Even that kid that is heading down the wrong path needs to hear some encouraging words sometimes. If I could not give these kids anything else, I tried to give them hope. I would look into the eyes of some of those students and I was able to tell that many of them were thirsty for knowledge. When most people get thirsty they drink water. When most people get hungry they eat food. But what happens when a person is hungry for knowledge and they don't know where to get it? What if they don't have that foundation that most of us have to seek out knowledge and other resources to help them succeed? When children are thirsty for knowledge and have that hungry desire to learn, if they are put into situations that hinder this growth and development they tend to lash out anyway they know how just to be seen or heard. This may explain the defiant behavior of some children in the home as well as in the school.

I wanted my students to pay very close attention to the words that I was delivering to them. As a way to get and keep their attention, I always wore my police uniform while I was teaching. The students would be very fascinated that a real police officer was in their class teaching. As a result, I would get bombarded with questions the entire fifty minute class period. I would probably answer forty to fifty questions per class. I did my best to try to answer all their questions, but I knew I had a lesson plan to teach. Sometimes I would stay late to answer questions they may have had during their lunch period. You can learn a lot about young people's issues and concerns by providing a platform by which they can talk freely. To all the educators out there in the world, I commend you for all your hard work and effort in educating the future of our country. Can you imagine what type of society we would have if everyone assumed the role of a teacher? If you pause and think for a moment, if you are one of the people who have climbed up the success ladder, you never would have made it without the help of a teacher. That teacher could have been in the school, church, at home, or in the shopping mall. Whatever the case, we all owe a teacher somewhere for how we turned out. They deserve all the credit.

"Officer Digby teaching character education to a group of elementary school children"

You don't need a college degree to teach children how they should live or treat one another. You don't need a college degree to demonstrate a high commitment to your family. You don't need a college degree to be a role model or a mentor. Some of my fondest mentors were men who had not spent a day in a college classroom. These men taught me something that cannot be taught in a traditional classroom. *Common Sense* . . .

To a greater extent, we are all teachers to someone whether we want to admit it or not. Teaching is a thankless but rewarding job. It is not one of those jobs that's done for the money. Your heart has to be in it. If your heart is not in it, you will be counterproductive. For those of you who are living right and doing the right thing, keep up the good work. Kids are visual just as adults. It is out inherent nature to believe what we see more so than what we hear. The language and vibes that your body sends off should speak for themselves. The greatest reward a teacher can receive is the day a former student credits him/her for helping them along the way. I remember a former student of mine whose name I can't remember. He was a black male, about seventeen years old, and he approached me in a store where I was working off duty in 2007. Our conservation went as follows:

> "Officer Digby, hello, do you remember me?" I stared at the young man who stood 6'2" looking me in my eyes and I replied, "I'm sorry I don't." The young man laughed and said, "That's OK." He then said to me, "Your teaching is a lot better than your memory." I laughed as we both stood there looking at each other for a few moments. He then went on to say, "Officer Digby, I beat the odds." I looked at the young man again trying to figure out where I knew this kid from. I just could not figure it out. I apologized to the young man and said, "I'm so sorry, I have taught so many students over the years that I can't remember them all." I then asked, "What odds did you beat?" He said, "I grew up in the hood and I refused to become a product of my own environment. I am on my way to Texas A&M University on a full scholarship." I told him that I was really excited for him and that I knew he would represent his hometown really well. He went on to say, "Officer Digby, I remember what you told our class six years ago. Character is who you really are not who others think you are. I am developing my own character now and I want to thank you."

"Why You Need To Be The Man"

Words could not express how I began to feel at that very moment. Here stood in front of me this young man that I had seen on three or four occasions in a classroom approximately six years earlier, and he remembered the words I said to his sixth grade class. Even more exciting, he was inspired to further his education and not be a product of his environment. This guy really made my day and I wish him all the luck in the world. I knew at that moment I had made a difference in not only his life, but perhaps the world.

My goal while teaching was to inspire, motivate, and cultivate every mind in the classroom. The only drawback was that I had only a few weeks and limited time to do this. Every time I got prepared to teach a new class, I would get excited with the questions from the inquisitive minds of these young bright students. The teachers also had questions of their own. I taught lesson plans on decision making, the importance of rules and laws, dealing effectively with peer pressure, and sometimes would just talk to my students about life in general. Sometimes, as a teacher you must be flexible enough to step away from the rigors of academics and talk to your students about what life is like in their world. I found this to be very helpful to me as well as opening up the lines of communications with my students. Once the word had gotten out among the students that I was approachable, they immediately began sharing with me their deepest thoughts and concerns, and they began to be the extra set of eyes police needed in their neighborhoods. Tapping into the minds of young people and watching them develop as they took in everything I said outweighed any profession I could ever work in. Establishing these informal relationships with teachers, staff, and students proved to be a valuable asset for the Dallas Police Department and the Dallas Independent School District. Combining my law enforcement career with education brought me joy unlike anything I could ever imagine.

I want to be clear. I am in no way saying that in order to help young people succeed you need to be a police officer. Law enforcement was the route I took to make a difference. You need to find your own. You need to find out what comes natural to you and what you have a passion for to make your impact felt. God has blessed us all with some amazing gifts. We are all unique; therefore, no two people are the same. Whatever gift God has blessed you with please find out what it is. Once you have determined what special gifts God has blessed you with, do the right thing and be a blessing to someone else.

As stated in chapter 1, we have seen some monumental changes in American history during the first decade of the twenty-first century. As a people, we can ill afford to get comfortable at this point. We all have work to do. The time to become concerned is when you think things are going well. We need to constantly stay on alert. We must be careful not to become complacent to the point that we feel we no longer need to stand and fight for something. Blacks have fought for civil rights, women have fought for equal rights, gay and lesbian couples are fighting to be recognized as married, but what about the rights of our children? Who is fighting for them? They can't fight for themselves, so who will take up the slack? The answer my friend is you!

I can't help but think about American civil rights activists Dr. Martin Luther King Jr. and Rosa Parks. Though the Montgomery, Alabama, bus boycott that started in 1955, and lasted over a year proved to be a historical event that helped shape the future of this country in terms of racial desegregation, what if MLK and Rosa had been content with that single movement? What if they had not realized that there was still more work to be done? What if they had decided to be reactive instead of continuing to be proactive through the strategic nonviolent movement? Would our lives have been different today? No matter what your skin color is, if the Civil Rights Movement had been stalled or eliminated, do you think America would be what it is today? If you had not realized it by now, on that December day in 1955, in Montgomery, Alabama, when Rosa Parks sat down on that bus seat and refused to give up her seat to a white man, she was really standing up for something much bigger. Rosa Parks was standing up for the right to be an American. Who would have thought that a single event such as this would have emerged to help shape American history? Rosa Parks and MLK used the events in Montgomery as a springboard to help launch the largest movement by a group of people in the history of the United States. We need not forget these people and the countless others before them who laid the foundation for the freedoms that America has today. The contributions of Parks, King, and thousands of others who were leaders have made our lives worth living. What are you willing to sacrifice for a better tomorrow? Are you willing to give all of yourself for the betterment of mankind? There is an old saying, "If you don't stand for something, then you will fall for anything."

Michael Baisden, a radio talk show host, syndicated in over seventy cities across the country, has been the voice of the people. Not just black people, but all people. The way he puts it, "Family, we need to sound the alarm. We cannot expect the policies made in the White House to take care of the problems we created in our house." Simply put, don't leave the burden of raising your kids to the politicians in Washington, DC. The government should not be telling you what to do in your own home unless you invite them in. If you are running your home like you are supposed to, government is not going to come knocking, wanting to know what is going on. We put the government in our lives, we allow the government in our homes, and when they dictate to us what they think should be done, then we get an attitude because it may go against our belief system.

The reason there is so much government intervention in our homes is because we have done a poor job at managing our own affairs. Because we have done a poor job at this, those good people in Washington, DC, think we need their help. In some cases we do. In most cases we don't. Government intervention is fine, but this alone will not conquer the problems that our youths are having whether they are black, white, or any other race. Please don't hold your breath if you are waiting for a magic formula from the U.S. Government to raise your kids. Raising children, especially boys, starts in the community and it has to start with real men stepping up. It is easy to sit back and point the finger. It is easy to blame all of our problems on the economy or the next-door neighbor. The reality of the matter is most of the problems that we have today did not occur overnight. Most of our problems with our children did not occur overnight. It is the result of poor planning, lack of decision making, lack of education, greed, and sometimes laziness that has almost brought this great country that we live in to its knees. High unemployment rates, teen pregnancies, an increase in the U.S. high school drop out rate, teen violence, teen suicide, and high incarceration rates especially for minorities just to name a few have many questioning what is going on in our communities. After so many years of progressive activities are we now starting to regress? It is easy to talk about what the problem is. The hard part is getting off your butts and doing something about it.

Being Lazy Can Kill Ya!

My parents taught me the benefits of hard work combined with passion at an early age. Laziness was never an issue in my household. I don't think I even knew how to spell the word until I was eleven years. I'm so thankful that my parents did not allow me to have too much idle time on my hands. When I was growing up, I spent most of my time doing things which were productive. I think this is one of the problems with our youths today. They have too much time to think about foolish things to get into. My parents would always tell me an idle mind is the devil's workshop. Laziness is like a cancer. Once you get a taste of it, it is hard to get rid of. Laziness is not a characteristic that is used to describe one's self. Instead, it takes someone else to notice your work ethic or lack thereof to come to the conclusion that you are lazy. Now don't get me wrong. We all have our moments when we do not feel like doing anything. I understand that. But how can one really tell if they are truly lazy? Here are a few questions you need to ask yourself to determine if you are lazy.

1. Am I the type of person who can't do anything for myself?
2. Do I always expect something for nothing?
3. Does everyone around me initiate all the activities that I engage in?
4. Do I lower my standards or self-worth for fear of hard work?
5. Am I willing to be just comfortable at all costs?
6. Do those who are close to me constantly remind me that I am lazy?

If you answer yes to any of these questions, you are probably a lazy person. The fact that you are reading this book is a good indicator that you are not a lazy person. You are probably the type of person that is or wants to be an agent of social change. People who tend to read these types of books tend to think proactively. To think proactively requires you to show some initiative. Lazy people are not proactive, nor, do they show a lot of initiative. If you are a lazy person, at this stage of the book you may want to put it down, because you won't get much out the chapters that follow. If you are a go-getter and are actively involved in your life and the lives of other children, by all means keep on reading; the best is yet to come.

You see, most lazy people don't read, and they lack proper information. To put it another way, lazy people read the wrong things. The mind is a very powerful tool. The mind is your most powerful asset. The lazy man only knows how to produce. He does not know how to define. Most people only utilize a fraction of their mental capacity and as a result a large part of your greatest asset goes unused. The mind must continue to be stimulated. When the day comes that you stop learning, then you stop living. Stimulate your mind by making lifestyle changes if you have not already done so. Start reading more books, journals, or magazines on things that can help elevate your thinking and put you in a position where you can live life on your terms. Thoughts are things. For whatever we tell our minds to do the body will follow.

Don't underestimate the power of young boys who watch their fathers reading books. This can be very powerful for a young person's development. Some men have the tendency to think they know everything about everything; therefore, they don't bother to read or study to try to research what somebody else has said on a certain topic. Why is it in today's society that when you go to a church, the congregation is mostly made up of women? Could it be that men, for the most part, have a problem with another man telling them what to do in their house? Why is it in the black community that more black women are going to college compared to black men? In the year 2000, a study was done which revealed that black men aged between eighteen and twenty-four are about two and a half times more likely than black women to go to jail as opposed to college. This is based on figures disclosed by the Census Bureau, which reveal that during the same time, seven hundred and forty seven thousand African American women in this age group were in college, while only nine thousand were in jail or prison. The number for their male counterparts claimed that only four hundred and eighty thousand young men were in college, while one hundred and eighty thousand were in jail or prison.

Are black men the least desired minority group in corporate America? If the answer is no, then we don't have a problem. If the answer is yes, then why is this the case? All of the questions posed above have some tough answers. I don't think there are any easy answers to any of these questions. I do know one thing. Individuals who lack initiative, are not self-starters, fail to complete a task, and always look for a way to escape are not only lazy but hazardous as well. I mean hazardous from the standpoint that people who have these types of characteristics seem to find it easy to attach themselves to people who are going places and who are actively pursuing dreams and goals. Hazardous people will bring you down. Stay away from people like this at all costs. Keep conversations to a minimal and keep your distance. The lazy person's only objective is to make sure that you don't accomplish anything that they themselves can't accomplish. People who have high energy are attracted to other people who have high energy. Have you ever been in a room full of people where you may not know any of them, but the vibe in the air just makes you feel good? It makes you say, "This is the place to be in." It is in your inherent nature to associate with people who are like you. If you are a go-getter and a self-starter you will draw strength from other people who think and function the same as you do.

Chapter 3

All Eyes On You

There is no doubt about it. Everybody is watching what everybody else is doing. There is no such thing as privacy anymore. Not even in your own home. Men are particularly in the limelight. Everybody has cell phones with cameras and video recorders on keychains alike. If you have been watching the media, men have taken up a lot of airtime with their adulteries making national news. In 2009, Tiger Woods, a husband, a father, and an athlete, was caught up in a sex scandal regarding him cheating on his wife. Several women came forward with their stories, alleging to have all slept with Woods. Woods and his family had to go through the public embarrassment and humiliation of Wood's actions. In 2008, former Democratic presidential candidate, John Edwards, made national news when it was alleged that he not only had an ongoing affair with another woman while he was married, but he also impregnated her. Edwards was more than untruthful to the American public. To make matters worse, Edwards' wife was suffering from a terminal illness, which really made Edwards appear to be spineless. In 2008, the story of former New York governor, Elliot Spitzer, made national headlines when it came out that he had mistresses in other countries, used tax dollars to spend time with them, and was an unfaithful husband. There are hundreds of cases like these that go unnoticed. The reason that these cases got national headlines was because of the positions that these men held.

Honestly, I did not think this was newsworthy. As far as I am concerned, any infidelity that occurs between a man and his wife is their business. Who am I to judge? Who are any of us to judge? The problem is that we put people up on this high pedestal and expect them to do no wrong. We put people in certain positions and expect them to be flawless. This is an unrealistic expectation, but it is alive and well. As men, we have to understand that whether we realize it or not, we demand a lot of attention. People watch the way you walk, they listen to the way you talk, they watch the way you dress, and they know what you love best. It is hard being a man in America. It is even harder being a black man. I approach being a black man in America the same way I approach a board game or any game that I am about to play for the first time. As with any game, the first thing you should do is *read the rules.* Have you ever tried to play a game without reading the rules? This would be a hard game to win. I'm here to tell you that if you play that game, you will never win. Everyday, young men get sucked into situations that are unwinnable. Take time to figure out just what direction you are heading in. Too often young men, especially black men, live in the moment. There is not much systematic thinking taking place. This is greatly hurting our young people, and those, with the life experience, need to intervene to get them on the right path.

Have you ever heard of a home-builder building a house without first looking at the site or the blueprint? Have you ever heard of someone who takes the driver's license test without first test-driving a car a few times with an experienced person and also studying the rules of the road? If they do take the test without proper preparation, they are destined to fail. Remember, if you fail to plan, you may as well plan on failing.

Hey, men, women are watching, your children are watching, and the world is watching. Life is one big game, and they are watching to see how well you play. However, it's not the type of game you can take lightly. The game of life requires *preparation,* which is the second thing you need. If you expect to gain anything positive from your experience on earth, it's going to require you to not only read, but also understand. President Barrack Obama did not wake up one morning and say to himself, "I want to be president of the United

"Why You Need To Be The Man"

States." The reason he is the commander in chief is because of the extensive preparation and guidance mixed with discipline, drive, charisma, and passion. The work that he has put in over the years helped build and shape him into the leader he is today. Years of planning and back-breaking work had to be done first or he never would have made it to where he is today. This is what a man is supposed to do.

Just as everyone else has their eye on men, it is important to understand how men view themselves. Elliott Liebow, in *Talley's Corner*, says thus:

> *The way in which the man makes a living and the kind of living he makes have important consequences for how the man sees himself and is seen by others; and these in turn, importunately shape his relationships with family members, lovers, friends, and neighbors. Making a living takes on an overriding importance at marriage. Although he wants to get married, he hedges his commitment from the very beginning because he is afraid not of marriage itself, but of his own ability to carry out his responsibilities as a husband and a father. His own father failed and had to "cut out" and the men he knows who have been or are married have also failed or are in the process of doing so. He has no evidence that he will not.*

Have you ever been in a place doing whatever it was you were doing and the little hairs on the back of your neck began to stand up? Or better yet, have you ever had to deliver a speech to a room full of strangers who were looking to you for answers to problems they are facing? What happens if there are too many questions and not enough answers? What happens if the group of people you are speaking to can see right through the fact that you are ill prepared and have no idea what you're talking about? Does any of this sound familiar? Let me bring this a little more closer to your living room. What if your own children have questions that they bring to you and you have no idea what to say or do?

I bet this has happened to every parent walking the face of this earth at least once. What did you do about it? How bad would it make you feel as a parent to have your young child ask you why you did something that you knew was wrong and would hurt other people? The worse thing a parent can do to a child is to look them in their eyes and lie to them. Of all the things that we teach our children, they will forget 80 percent of it. But I guarantee you, they will remember the one lie you told them twenty years after the fact, with no help whatsoever.

Children have this inherent ability to recall events and situations that at the end of the day nobody cares about but them. Think about all the things children must be taught how to do. Children must be taught how to drive. They must be taught how to study. They must be taught how to use good manners and so on. The one thing children do not have to be taught is how to lie. A child will figure out at a relatively young age how they can manipulate a situation in their favor to get what they want.

You would be amazed at the number of people in this world who say their greatest fear is public speaking. Some of the greatest public speakers of the twentieth century were strong, powerful black men. On August 28, 1963, Martin Luther King Jr. delivered one of the most powerful speeches of the twentieth century. His speech "I Have A Dream," inspired an entire nation that we needed change now and could ill afford to wait any longer, as two hundred and fifty thousand people from across the nation fled to Washington DC to see this man move a nation with his powerful words. In his book, *Why We Can't Wait*, MLK said, "To give a man a pair of shoes without first teaching him how to walk is cruel. We need a powerful sense of determination to banish the ugly blemish of racism scarring the image of America." Malcolm X, who was a leading figure in the twentieth century movement for black liberation in the United States, used his words to speak volumes during the period of the Civil Rights Movement. Bill Cosby, the comedian, actor, and author who has publicly announced his dissatisfaction with our youths, and has written books on fatherhood and life, also falls into the category of the twentieth century's most prominent speakers.

My day job at times has required me to give public presentations to large groups of people in various settings. I have had to speak to community leaders and special interest groups on crime trends in their communities. I've had to give presentations to high school and college-age students in classrooms on what they need to be doing to increase the chances of them being successful as they prepare for the next transition in life. I spend a lot of my time talking to elementary-school-age children, teaching them the importance of good character and why they need to strive to become good citizens.

It really motivates me when I'm in front of a large classroom, full of young minds that are all eager to learn, and they just want someone to inspire and encourage them. When I teach classes on character education, I always advise my students that the information I give them goes far beyond the walls of the classroom. I want to plant deep-seeded roots in the minds of young people that failure is not an option. I define character as "who you really are, not who others think you are." In other words, what would you really do if you thought nobody was looking? Who others think you are is not your true character. Who others think you are is your reputation. Which one do you think is most important? They both play integral parts in our development as we go through this journey called life. First, let's look at character.

Character

Your character is your internal makeup. Your character is a combination of your morals, values, and upbringing. According to former NFL Head Coach Tony Dungy, "Your character is tested, revealed, and further developed by the decisions we make in the most challenging times. We have to know what is right, and we have to choose to do it. That is how character is developed—by facing those decisions and choosing the right way over and over until it becomes second nature. It's just how you do things." With all of this mixed together you come up with a unique person unlike nobody else. When you think of your own character, you should ask yourself, "Can I sleep at night and rest easy with the decision I am about to make?" People who believe in a high degree of integrity and have character find it increasingly difficult to lie and cheat themselves through life because they know they are held accountable to a much higher power. Your word is your bond. People with a high degree of character are not overly concerned with looking good as they are with doing what's right. When people who value their character are wrong and they realize they are wrong, they are quick to apologize.

Character has to be built from the inside out. Trying to build character from the outside and then put it inside you is like spraying on cologne without first taking a bath. The end result being, it does not look or smell good. The following are the examples of questions I ask children: Would you take the answer key off your teacher's desk for an upcoming test if you had the chance? Would you be willing to lie to get ahead and sacrifice your creditability? If you saw someone drop their wallet on the floor in a department store and you picked it up and it had $400 inside, would you try to catch that person and advise them that they just dropped their wallet? Would you be willing to steal that piece of candy or clothing from the store shelf if you thought you could get away with it? You would be surprised that some of the answers I got were very interesting.

The reason why some of these answers were interesting was because all of the children had different definitions of character and they had a different value system based upon their upbringing. The reason why the concept of character is misunderstood by children is because often times it is misunderstood by adults. I have asked adults such questions as the following: If you saw someone drop money on the ground would you pick it up and give it back to them? Would you gamble on your families' future to satisfy a personal goal that in the end will only benefit you? Many young people have no idea where the word *character* comes from or what it really means. If a person does not know what a word means or where it comes from, how do we expect them to put it in practical application of life?

Many young people have nobody to instill in them good positive character traits. Traits such as honesty, integrity, and dependability are lost. Men, let's step up our game. We need to do a better job at teaching our children right from wrong. We need to give our children a sense of responsibility, but it has to begin with us first. Let's please stop leaving this task up to women. Guys, they can neither do it alone, nor, should they be expected to. They need us to mentor, guide, motivate, inspire, and instill greatness in our children. Men, we are here to lead by example. Now I know that some men may need an education in this area themselves. If that is the case, it is OK. But you have to realize that and educate yourself. We need to get serious about our jobs, and I don't mean the one you go to from 8:00 a.m. to 5:00 p.m. Hey, men, our kids are watching us, and we need to take notice. All eyes are on you. You remember that.

Hey, men, let me tell you all something. Your community is watching, the media is watching, your spouse is watching, and most of all your children are watching how you handle everything in your life whether it is good or bad. Men, we are under the microscope. Our children need role models, and we need to be there for them. You may have several jobs throughout your lifetime and you may even be successful at many of them. There is one job that you cannot afford to be a failure at. That job is being a man and being a father. If we fail at being men and fathers, the consequences will be deadly for our children.

Pictured: Samuel Digby and infant daughter Jasmin in May 2002.

Our children are dropping out of high school at record rates. In Texas, one out of three students are dropping out of high school. Teenage pregnancy in the United States is at an all-time high, the penal institution is overcrowded with services now being contracted out to private corporations, sadly, we are losing our children to senseless violence on the streets of America, teen suicide is at an all-time high, and the list can go on and on. I was once asked by a young lady on a college campus, "Where should character classes be taught?" My initial response to her was, "I believe that the first place a character course should be taken is the home and the purpose of the school should be to reinforce what the child is being taught in the home." If we expect our schools to do anymore than this, especially if we are not doing our parts in the home, then disappointment is right around the corner. Here are a few things that we all can do to help develop our character. Though this list is not exhaustive, it is however, a starting point:

1. Develop a closer relationship with God
2. Learn to become a better student
3. Appreciate the talents and special gifts of those around you
4. Don't be afraid to stand alone for what is right
5. When appropriate speak your mind and voice your opinion
6. Don't be easily persuaded
7. Become a cheerful giver and always give more than you receive
8. Assume positions to demonstrate your ability to lead others
9. Read as many books as you can
10. Exercising your body is just as important as exercising your mind
11. Think positive thoughts as this often leads to positive actions
12. Listen more than you talk (You have two ears and one mouth for a reason)
13. Strive to develop your success through helping other people achieve theirs.
14. Become involved in issues affecting your community
15. Become and continue to be an advocate for education
16. Let people see the fun side of you sometimes
17. Learn to have more patience in your life and be patient with those around you. Especially your children

18. Become a mentor to some young person
19. Don't spread rumors, good or bad
20. Most of all, don't be indecisive. Demonstrate your ability to make sound decisions.

Reputation

The younger a person is, the more concerned that person is about their reputation. Older people tend to place more value on their character. Your character is just like your retirement account. The earlier you start on it the better off you will be in the long run. I don't want to downplay the importance of reputation as it relates to character. Reputation is important. The problem is that many people have compromised their character for a better reputation. If you only work on your reputation and never visit your character, any success you may have will be short lived.

You have to be in touch with both in order to be effective and successful. Remember what we said reputation is? Your reputation is who others think you are. Many people live in this little glass bubble, and when they step outside of this glass bubble, they are ashamed of the true them. They ask themselves such questions as what will my neighbors think? What will my teammates say? How will my colleagues react? What will the church say? Now your reputation is important in the sense that we all want people to recognize our good deeds without us having to explain ourselves all the time. We all want our work to speak for itself. Men by nature tend to be prideful. Men like to be acknowledged for hard work, dedication, or accomplishment of goals. In order to continue to be acknowledged, you must demonstrate your level of competence in an area over and over again. By doing this you develop the reputation of someone who knows what they are doing and can be trusted.

You will establish your reputation first and foremost. However, after your reputation has been established, it will only take a little while before your true character starts to come out. At some point, you want your character and reputation to match up together. If these two don't match, you will be like a glass window, in that everyone will be able to see right through you. The following is a true story of a good friend of mine.

It Started Right and Ended Wrong

A friend of mine, in his early thirties, was working his way up the corporate ladder. He was a corporate attorney, working for a prestigious law firm. His ultimate goal when he came to the firm was to become a partner. He had been an associate for seven years in this law firm and had won 92 percent of his cases. He had the highest winning percentage of any attorney in the firm. He had earned the respect of other associates as well as the other partners. This young attorney had made this firm millions of dollars during his tenure. He had attracted some major accounts worldwide and had become a valued asset to this firm.

This young attorney felt that he had gone far and beyond his duty to demonstrate his commitment and dedication to this firm. Finally, the day came that this young aspiring attorney had long been waiting for, since he joined the firm. One of the senior partners in the firm had retired; therefore, a partner position became available immediately. He interviewed for the position and everyone in the firm spoke very highly of his work ethic. Even the other associates, who interviewed for the partner position, recommended him for the position of partner because of his qualifications and the hard work he had displayed over the years. This attorney had built the reputation of being a go-getter and a hard charger and did not let anything stand in his way of winning a case. This attorney was lethal in the courtroom. As a matter of fact, when other attorneys in the city found out that he would be trying a case, they quickly tried to settle out of court.

The reputation this attorney had built up for himself was astonishing. He knew that his work would speak for itself, so he approached the interview with the other partners with confidence. Over the course of the interview, the other partners were very impressed with the applicant. However, there was one partner in the room who was not quite convinced that this attorney was the person they were looking for to add to their ranks. One of the partners said to my friend, "I see that you have been quite successful, and you have been quite an asset to this firm. I'm just wondering, what are you willing to sacrifice to win a case?" My friend replied, "Anything I have to do to win, I will do." My friend answered the question in the way he thought the other partners wanted him to answer. My friend defined himself as a man only by what he did in the courtroom. There was no other gauge he used to measure his manhood.

My friend used an example of a case that the firm took in which he was the lead counsel two years earlier. During the course of the case, he determined that the client had deliberately hid assets, was untruthful to the court, and engaged in criminal activity. My friend, knowing that the case was a fraud, defended his client and recovered a huge settlement as a result. Many people were adversely affected as a result of this settlement. The partners then asked my friend, "How did that make you feel?" My friend replied, "Great! it was a good win for me and a good win for the firm." The partners then ended the interview by shaking my friend's hand and advising him that they would be in touch to let him know their decision. They shook hands and my friend got up from his seat and left the conference room.

After an extensive debate among the partners that lasted almost two weeks, they determined that my friend was not who they were looking for to join them at the top of the firm. You see, based on the responses he gave, the other partners all agreed that he had a questionable character, which could easily be compromised. Furthermore, even though my friend had a great reputation throughout the firm and was indeed an asset, he was a man of very little character and integrity, which the other partners viewed as being a huge liability. This firm put a premium on honesty and integrity of their associates, and in their eyes my friend lacked that. In the end, his character and reputation were not lining up together.

Sometimes people must be willing to make the right decision instead of the most popular decision. This also demonstrates true leadership. In the case above, the most popular decision cost my friend big time. He thought that what he was doing was a good thing. It goes back directly to his internal makeup or his character. After my friend got the news that he was not going to be selected for the partner position, he was distraught for the next several weeks. He ended up leaving the firm and taking another position on the other side of town for half the pay. It became painfully clear to him that no amount of money was worth his integrity, and he never again wanted this aspect of his life questioned again.

When I hear of stories like the one above, I can't help but wonder did the ends justify the means? I truly believe that my friend's heart was in the right place. He did what he thought in his mind he was supposed to do. But in the end, it backfired. This is a common practice in organizations. I have seen people move up in their respective organizations quite fast and step on many heads on their way up to the top. The end result, when they make it to the top, is that they quickly find out that they have no supporters and they come tumbling down the organization as quickly as they rose up.

CHAPTER 4

The Three Ds Of Manhood

Now that we have discussed that actions speak louder than words and that everybody is watching you, let us press on to some other dimensions that are crucial for manhood development. Chris Gardner, the author of *The Pursuit of Happyness* and *Start Where You Are* talks about the struggles that life dealt him and his young son while he was striving to make it in the corporate world. He stated,

> *It's often much easier to stay in our comfort zones, even when we've stopped being comfortable, simple because it takes less effort to stay where we don't want to be than to summon the energy required to create the change to go where we'd rather be. I have learned that change is necessary for growth, and that if we don't instigate the change that we desire for ourselves, the status quo will eventually change on its own-in ways that can make adapting even tougher.*

For those that are struggling with being lazy and trying to get the energy necessary to start down that road of success, both of Chris Gardner's books are a must-read. This chapter identifies the three Ds, which, I think, are the dimensions instrumental for young boys transforming into manhood. The three Ds are discipline, dedication, and determination. Let's talk about discipline first.

Discipline

Discipline. What does this word *discipline* really mean? I'm willing to bet that if I put fifty people in a room and interviewed each one separately, they would all give me fifty different definitions of the word *discipline*. Are you one of those people who always start something and never finish it? Have you ever heard of that saying, "Birds of a feather flock toge*ther?*" People who lack self-discipline don't hold themselves accountable, and they attract other people who lack self-discipline and are not accountable. Don't you dare be one of those type of men!

Let me tell you my definition of *discipline*. Discipline, simply stated, is the ability to implement self-control over the decision-making process. Discipline is a concept that has to be taught. One is not somehow born a disciplined person. It is in our inherent nature to want things right away and not put it off for a later date. It is in our inherent nature to want to take shortcuts, cut corners, or get the hook up. The concepts of hard work and delayed self-gratification are no longer part of the American way. Isn't this why we now have the interest-only home loans, the credit cards with $6,000 credit balances on 28 percent APR, the subprime lenders who get people into these ridiculous home mortgages at 9 percent and higher, and the adjustable rate mortgages, which has resulted in the highest number of foreclosures in U.S. history? None of these facts I have just stated are news to your ears or eyes. As a result of all this instant gratification, we are promoting an entire generation of young people with the entitlement mentality. Entitlement can be defined as something for nothing. As a civilized group of people, we no longer improvise discipline over the things that we do daily. If you don't think so, take a look at this. Look at the credit card and housing crisis we currently have in the United States. Fifty—percent of Americans are in debt due to overspending, which stems from lack of discipline. We get ourselves into situations that we expect others to bail us out of. To be disciplined means to plan for the unexpected. Have you ever tried planning for an emergency during an emergency? It does not work too well, does it? But, what about planning for the bad times when things are good? I promise you, if you get into a habit of being proactive in all aspects of

"Why You Need To Be The Man"

your life, when an emergency does arise, what you will find out is that it really is not an emergency. This takes an enormous amount of discipline.

Americans have a hard time saying no. The times we are living in now dictate that we acquire things instantaneously without methodically thinking about the consequences of our actions. Think for a moment about a small newborn baby that is just coming into the world. His/her only way of communicating is by crying. As parents, we don't want our children to cry, so we do whatever we need to do to comfort the baby. However, as time goes by, that baby becomes a toddler and then a small child. During this process, a certain amount of training needs to be taking place.

A child has to be taught that he/she no longer can have what they want when they want it. Tough love has to kick in. Is this mean? I don't think so. You are simply teaching your child the discipline he/she needs to handle disappointment as they will have many disappointments throughout the course of their lives. Children who are not taught this become spoiled brats. Even worse, when they become adults, and have never been disciplined as children, they end up being useless products, becoming burdens on society. Dr. W. E. B. DuBois in *The Souls of Black Folk*, said, "To stimulate wildly weak and untrained minds is to play with mighty fires, to flout their striving idly is to welcome a harvest of brutish crime and shameless lethargy in our very laps. The guiding of thought and the deft coordination of deed is at once the path of honor and humanity." DuBois believed that the key to equality and evening of the playing field for black men with mainstream America was education.

Being disciplined does not necessarily mean you will never be able to have a particular item. Being disciplined does not always have to hurt. It may just mean that you can't have that particular item right now. In due time, it may be more of an option. Give yourself time to grow, develop, and mature into a self-conscious, disciplined man. Educate yourself and recognize your deficiencies. Believe me when I tell you that nothing attracts a woman more than a self-conscious man who is secure with himself and can handle the adversities that life throws at him steadfastly.

Are men viewed as the more disciplined sex? I will leave that question for you to answer at some other time. Men are not supposed to be impulsive at anything. Men are thinkers. Men are doers. Men are analytical by nature. With that said, we are supposed to have enough self-control to not overreact and to think rationally. With all this said, have we lived up to this standard? If we fail to live up to this standard, how in the world can we expect anything greater from our children? Remember in the chapter 3, all eyes are on you. According to Ayanna G in her article "Why Do More Black Women Attend College Than Black Men?" she stated,

> *Single black mothers sometimes spoil their sons more than their daughters. This may be because some mothers claim that raising girls is more difficult than raising boys. The assumption is that boys need less attending to. This results in less structure, and less structure means less discipline. And discipline is a necessity where it regards higher education.*

Jawanza Kunjufu, in *The Conspiracy To Destroy Black Boys,* said, "The factors that contribute to the decline in African American boys' achievement are 1) a decline in parental involvement, 2) an increase in peer pressure, 3) a decline in nurturance, 4) a decline in teacher expectations, 5) a lack of understanding of learning styles, and 6) a lack of male teachers." Mr. Kunjufu believes the term "at risk" is too popular. Mr. Kunjufu stated, "When we use the term 'at risk,' we need to look at the institutions and the factors that caused this child to be at risk."

People are watching and waiting in anticipation of your every move. This is especially the case with your children. I put such an emphasis on the children because I have a vested interest in the development of every child. The words that men speak to their children or any child they are in constant contact with will do one of two things: either the words will build them up or tear them down. As men, we demand a lot of attention from all who are around us. Have you ever noticed that when a man hits rock bottom, everybody knows about it. When a woman does the same thing, she manages to keep things going and no matter how hard things get the people who are closest to her still don't know what's going on until the last minute. Think for a moment how society views an unemployed man versus an unemployed woman. Though both are not good situations to be in, there is considerably more pressure on a man to make things happen. When men can't make things happen for themselves or their families, society questions their manhood. Truth be told, men begin to question their own manhood. Is this fair? Women, on the other hand, are not subjected to the same pressures that men are subjected to by society. Women have a different set of issues that they must deal with that men know nothing about. I'm not saying that women's problems are less important, I'm just saying that women have a different set of issues to deal with than men.

Many of our goals and dreams fall short because we lack the proper discipline to execute them. All discipline means is that you are willing to stay the course no matter what. You must be willing to do what the next man is not willing to do. You must be willing to go where the next man is not willing to go. You must be willing to do what most people would consider impossible. This is your quest to establish disciplined growth. Discipline at time requires each of us to sacrifice our time and energy. The key to remember is that the ends must justify the means. The proper mind-set is the key to becoming and staying disciplined. Dreams are nothing more than goals with a deadline. In your route to becoming a more disciplined man you need to do a few things along the way.

1. Establish an achievable goal
2. Internalize the goal. Create a vision
3. Create an action plan for your goal
4. Put your goal into execution
5. Share your goal and the experience of acquiring it

1. Establish An Achievable Goal

Life is made up of several battles that need to be conquered along the way. The United States did not win the Revolutionary War with one battle. Several battles had to be won before victory was declared. The fight for civil rights was not won with one battle. Several small battles had to be won before the Civil Rights Act of 1964 became law. The success of United States in World War II was not a result of one air strike and one battle won. This war was won through strategic planning and execution of the troops on the ground. Too often, young men go for the knockout punch without wearing the enemy down. The enemy in some cases is society.

In the sport of boxing, very few fights have been won in the first round with one punch. Even if a fight is won in the first round, it usually requires the boxer to throw several different combinations of punches that the opponent does not expect. This can catch the opponent off guard. A smart boxer trains and prepares for a fight that goes all fifteen rounds. He does not cut corners because he figures that he is better than his opponent. He trains for months in anticipation that this fight will go the distance. The smart boxer trains for that ultimate moment that all fighters try to avoid: being knocked out themselves. If, when he gets into the ring and he lands a few good blows to his opponent that knocks him out, that's great. He has not lost anything. He has been prepared mentally and physically to do battle. If by chance, he is not prepared to go the distance, anticipating a quick win by a knockout, and the fight goes the distance, he puts himself at a considerable disadvantage because he is ill prepared. Life is the same way. As men, especially black men, we are all in a fight for our lives just as a boxer is in the boxing ring. If we fail to properly train for our fight, we too can get knocked out. The problem with this is that if you get knocked out of this fight called life, you may never recover from your injury. And if you do recover, sometimes the damage that has been done is so severe, that you will live a marginal life at best.

Young men need to have small short-term goals that are realistic to obtain. Setting your standards too high too soon will cause nothing more than becoming discouraged. For example, a young person in high school may have aspirations of becoming a medical doctor one day. Anyone in this field knows that this is not a process that occurs overnight. It takes years of planning, commitment, and skills to get to this point. A short-term goal that this student may have could be to become involved in extracurricular activities at his/her school to familiarize themselves with various avenues they can pursue in the medical profession to give them that early exposure. Another short-term goal may be for him/her to seek summer employment in doctors' offices, hospitals, or health care facilities. Another short-term goal may be to graduate high school and purse a pre-med degree from a university that has strong programs in the sciences. All of these short-term victories, together with discipline will accomplish the overall goal of becoming a doctor. Achieving short-term wins with accomplishing goals that are attainable gives individuals the confidence they need to continue to set new goals. Remember, you're in a fight for your life. You cannot accept a tie or a draw. You must win and win convincingly. This is very important. These are the rules to this game called life.

2. Internalize Your Goal. Create A Vision

Your goals need to become part of you. Once your goals have been clearly identified and established, you need to visualize yourself completing each one. As adults we need to teach our children that the greatest monster in life is staring at them every morning when they wake up and look in the mirror. In this world, your biggest competitor should be yourself. Your greatest critic should be yourself. There is nothing better than a self-evaluation from time to time. Failure is not an option. If you think it is, let me refer you to the late great pop icon Michael Jackson who wrote a song years ago called, "Man in the Mirror." I believe that this song will stand the test of time. This song spoke volumes about many people's lives, and in my opinion, it is one of the greatest songs ever recorded. I listen to this song over and over again because Michael Jackson had a message in this song that we all needed to be reminded of everyday. In one verse, Michael Jackson says, "If you want to make the world a better place takes a look at yourself and make that change." It is a very powerful message in this song and one that needs to be engraved in the minds of all our young people. If you have not heard "Man in the Mirror," you need to. It is truly life changing.

If given the opportunity, the greatest gift you can give a child is the opportunity to dream. Give young people the opportunity to dream about what can be. Once children figure out what can be, they can then focus their attention on what ought to be. The problem with many children today is that they lack vision. To tell the truth, many adults lack vision. Without a vision, you are going nowhere really fast. My definition of vision is the ability to look beyond tomorrow, beyond next week, or even beyond ten years from now to seek out your destiny and define your purpose in life. Visionaries don't make decisions that have an impact only on tomorrow. Their decisions and the lives they live have an impact on generations to come.

3. Create An Action Plan For You Goal

The question was asked in an earlier chapter: Have you ever heard of a house being built without a blueprint? Here is another question that I think would apply: Have you ever heard of any team, whether it is baseball, basketball, football, or hockey, winning a championship without plays already drawn up? The point is at this stage of the game, goals have been established and visualized, and now you need to put your goals into action. That old saying "actions speak louder than words" speaks volumes in this step. In this step, it involves you getting around people who can assist you with making your goal their priority and making it a part of a larger agenda. Now I know not all goals will meet this requirement. It is hopeful that as you attain one goal, which may be of lesser importance to someone else, and as you attain the next goal and the goal after that the value of each goal increases, making them more of a priority to someone else. An action plan for your goals also means that someone will be holding you accountable, making sure these goals are met and are being executed. This is not a bad thing. Again there is no better feeling than knowing that somebody is talking about what you've got going on.

Retired Police Chief David Kunkle of the Dallas Police Department comes to mind as I think of an action plan. Prior to Chief Kunkle taking over command of the Dallas Police Department in 2004, he stated that his goal was to reduce crime and increase police moral. As part of his action plan, Chief Kunkle hired over seven hundred new police officers, gave six promotional exams to allow officers to move up in the organization, opened a new patrol division, established the W. W. Caruth Jr. Police Institute at Dallas, and got officers certification pay up to an extra $500 per month. As a result, crime rate was down by 30 percent for the sixth straight year, and police moral also greatly improved, resulting in improved relationships with the community.

Chief Kunkle exceeded his initial goal, and his leadership and tenacity have left the city of Dallas and the Dallas Police Department in better shape than it was when he took over in 2004. This is the type of thing that adds to your self-worth.

4. Put Your Goals Into Execution

Methodical planning is the key to the overall success of your goals. You have to be willing to get off your butt and make things happen. Your goals will never just fall out of the sky and land in your lap. If it is a future politician's goal to run for and eventually win a public office, he/she must be ready to do some serious legwork. This may mean getting out and attending special interest events. It may even involve attending churches in different cross sections of the town. Going door to door in neighborhoods where the citizens have a lack of trust for government and the political system may be necessary. More importantly, these are things that should be done after the election is over, if reelection is a part of the future plans. Finding and supporting an important agenda that you are passionate about and that is also a hot political subject is beneficial. All of these and more would be necessary if success is the ultimate goal.

In order for the goals that are being executed to be meaningful, it involves plenty of energy on your part. There is a rite of passage that we all must take in achieving our goals. Just because somebody else has accomplished a goal that you also want to accomplish does not mean it's your time. In the process of putting your goals into execution, you must know and understand your limitations. For example, a five-foot seven-inch person will probably never become a center in the NBA. No matter how hard they practice, no matter what their skill level is, the likelihood of them becoming a center in the NBA is highly unlikely. He has no control over how tall he grows. Especially since the average height of a center in the NBA is seven feet. Learn how to concentrate your efforts on things that are directly within your control. Do not spend too much time on things that have no meaning and on which you have no control. At the end of the day, you will be very disappointed.

It is incumbent upon all of us that we map out the paths we take in achieving our goals. This is very important because we are all just one decision away from a catastrophe ourselves. Most working-class people are just one paycheck away from being homeless. If we turn left where we should have turned right, it could have serious consequences, and you may not have a second chance again. With this said, you must try to predict the overall outcome and plan accordingly. The success-minded person always incorporates a certain degree of failure while orchestrating his plan. In doing so, he comes up with a contingency plan to put in place in the event the master plan fails. A contingency plan is nothing more than an alternative plan or a backup plan, should the original plan fail to go through. Sometimes your contingency plan can be just a simple modification of your master plan. Sometimes you may plan something and things happen better than what you had planned. On the other hand, don't put all your eggs in one bucket. In the financial world they refer to this as diversification. Smart investors would never think about putting all of their money in one type of stock. If they did that and the economy took a turn for the worst, the investor would lose everything. So why would you hang all of your goals on the same coat hanger? If you did that and the coat hanger broke, everything you had on the hanger would fall to the floor.

5. Share Your Goals And The Experience Of Acquiring Them

You don't become educated about a subject matter and sit on that education and not share what you learned. This would be very selfish. The way you share your goals and experience is by mentoring and teaching. I said in earlier chapters, that each of us must use every moment as a teaching moment to help our children become all they can be. We are all different and unique in our own little way. God made us this way so that we can depend on one another. There is nothing more satisfying than sharing your experience with someone who is following in your footsteps. You have experience and knowledge right now inside of you, and there is somebody somewhere that is waiting for you to inspire them with your wisdom. Inspire a child today.

Dedication

When you are dedicated to something, you actually become pretty good at it. You are dedicated to your careers, community projects, friends, social groups, and a list of other things that at the end of your life won't matter. What about your dedication to your families? As men, collectively over the last twenty-plus years, we have failed in this area dramatically. Can you imagine the result if this intense energy that you put into the workplace, a project, or program was put into your marriage and family? What type of husband or father would you be then? What type of citizen would you be? What type of world would we have? How do you think your children will respond when they know where Daddy's top priority is? Who do you think would give your children the love and understanding of a father the way you would? As men, we must ensure that we send our children out into the world prepared to deal with the challenges that this world brings with it. We cannot afford to have our children in a dumbfounded state. It's our job to get them ready. If it was up to me, I would advocate school all year around for grades K through 12. I am an advocate for education. They are going to school all year around in countries like China and Japan. Children overseas are being prepared for this ever-changing global economy. It's not enough just to be great at your school or the best in the neighborhood. We need to make sure that our children think outside the box and recognize the fact that their competition exceeds the borders of the United States.

I want you to think for a moment where you spend most of your time. After you think about where you spend most of your time, I want you to then ask yourself, "Am I satisfied?" If the answer is yes, that's great. If the answer is no, that's still great. The fact remains that wherever you spend most of your time and whomever you are with is where your true dedication lies. If you spend most of your time gambling, then you are a gambler. This is something that is very important to you, and at all costs you need to place that bet. If you spend most of your time in bars, drinking alcohol as a coping mechanism, then you probably are an alcoholic. If you spend most of your time trying to make others around you better, loving your family, and sharing all that you have to offer, then you are probably a decent human being. You are who you associate with. If you hang around a group of losers, then you are no better than they are. Conversely, if your friends are successful and productive citizens, then you too will reap benefits from their great company.

Think for a moment the work that a farmer does. A farmer's primary job is to plant a seed. He plants a seed with the hope that one day it will be harvest time. He never really knows for sure if the seed that is planted will produce a positive result, but he plants the seed anyway because farmers are proactive. The farmer never knows for sure the course that nature will take. The point is the farmer does not just plant a seed and forget about it. After the seed is planted, the soil has to be nourished. The foundation has to be cared for. It has to be checked on and given consistent attention. If this is not done, the farmer risks damaging the crop, and it will not be useful to him or anyone else. A farmer knows that there are many who depend on his crop. So he feels an obligation not only to his family, but also to people abroad. Finally after months of planting and growth, the seed that was planted produces a crop by which the farmer can live and raise his family. This crop then ends up on the shelves of grocery stores all across the country to feed other families. People have benefited from this farmer's hard work. This process could not have been made possible if the farmer lacked the dedication necessary to accomplish this. The crop that is produced is much like a child. A child is nothing more than a seed that needs to be nourished, mentored, and programmed so that one day he/she grows up to be a productive individual where not only his family benefits, but society benefits as well. Are you giving your best?

The Dedicated Angel

In March 1997, I was preparing to complete my third year of college. I had worked hard all year long, had maintained my status on the Dean's List, and life was going pretty well for me. Many people say that some schools are more "party" schools than others. I say, the geographic location of a college does not matter. Whenever you put together a large group of young adults between the ages of eighteen and twenty-three, there is going to be a party somewhere all the time. The key is if you are a student then give yourself a reason to celebrate. Study hard and earn the grade that you are suppose to earn and if time permits, party on the weekend.

I had a good friend of mine who studied criminal justice with me in college, and he was scheduled to graduate May 1997. My friend was a classy type of a guy and known throughout the campus as strong-willed and dedicated. He never had a negative word to say about anyone. He was active in the student government body on the campus and had strong political views advocating social programs in the inner city. The stance he took on social policy, along with the above average grades he had received during his four years in college, earned him a full scholarship to study law at one of this nation's top law schools. Everyone knew that he was going to be something special in the future. Then tragedy struck.

One spring night in March 1997, there was a house party not far from the campus. Most college parties are safe because the worse thing college students may do to each other at a party is fight. They don't kill each other. On this tragic night, a fight broke out between some students at the party and some local fellows from the neighborhood. These local hoodlums had nothing to do with the university or anybody at the party. As the fight escalated, the local guys were forced to leave. The party ended shortly thereafter at which point many people were on the streets, walking back to campus and to their vehicles. All of a sudden a series of gunshots ranged out. Pow pow pow! was the noise that caused panic. The crowd scattered through the streets in a frenzy trying to take cover. Whoever said that a bullet does not have a name on it must have had my friend in mind, because he caught one round in the neck. On top of the people running trying to take cover, there was another group of students in a frenzy, trying to help my wounded friend. All the love and praying in the world could not save him. This was another senseless act of violence in the black community that has destroyed several families. My friend had nothing to do with the disturbance that occurred earlier in the evening. He just happened to be in the wrong place at the wrong time. The perpetrator that fired the fatal shot was a seventeen-year-old kid. Mad because of an issue he had with someone in the party earlier, he waited until the party was over and started shooting into a crowd of people, as they walked down the street. Fortunately, nobody else was struck. Unfortunately, the life of a black man, whom I knew would one day change the world, was cut short at the hands of another black man. We will never know what was going on through the mind of the young man who pulled that trigger. One thing that we do know is that this is not a new issue, and it happens all to frequently in the black community. God has an angel in heaven with my friend now, and I am sure he is looking down on all of us that knew him, as we continue the legacy that he lived for.

Determination

Are you a determined individual? Do you have what it takes to stand the course? People who have that determined spirit will let nothing stand in their way of achieving their goal. Having the proper mind-set is the key to overcoming obstacles. I can remember the determination I had while pursing my undergraduate degree at Tennessee State University. During my time as an undergraduate, I had the opportunity to meet many people from all walks of life. There were, however, only a few individuals that I established relationships with that have blossomed into lifelong friendships. These men are model citizens and I am honored to say that I know them and that they are truly my friends. They are Anthony and Ken.

The Motivators Voice

My friend Anthony was another individual who inspired me to go into the law enforcement profession. During our college years, we spent every evening in the library, studying and trying to always stay ahead. Anthony led the study groups most of the time. Every night from 7:00 p.m. to 10:30 p.m., Anthony, Ken, and I would meet in the library. The only reason we did not meet was if something was wrong with us due to an illness or if one of us got tied up at work. The study groups proved to be so beneficial that other students from the criminal justice department noticed our progress and wanted to meet and study with us. This study group turned into a great networking tool. This was all fine and good until we got over seven students in our group, because then studying was no longer conducive. When people try to do something good, it only takes one person to get everyone off task. Anthony, who primarily led our study sessions, noticed that this was occurring, therefore, we had to break the study group into two groups of four to get back on task.

Anthony and Ken were a few years older than I, and this was a tremendous advantage for me. I learned a great deal from these men inside the classroom as well as outside. Anthony is a police officer and has worked his way up to the rank of police sergeant at his agency. I remember when Anthony graduated from Tennessee State University in May 1997, and his demeanor was that of someone who was full of pride and self-confidence. He entered academy training later on that summer and began his law enforcement career. But what impressed me the most about Anthony was that even after he had graduated from college and had started going through police academy training, he still made his way back to the university to meet with Ken and I at 7:00 p.m. to study, just as we had done for the past three years. This was dedication at its finest. Anthony was not only dedicated, but he was determined to make sure that we were held accountable and that we were successful. He clearly demonstrated this by making sure we stayed on top of our studies and checking with us to see if there was anything he could do to help us gain more practical understanding of the subject matter. Anthony, at times, would bring some of his police-recruit classmates to these study sessions and they would be used as actors for our role-play scenarios. This also proved to help me develop a closer relationship with the law enforcement community, which was a career path that I eventually chose about a year and a half after Anthony graduated from Tennessee State. Anthony made sure we stayed on track and did not lose focus of why we were at Tennessee State University in the first place. Anthony's presence alone made me want to be better, and there was so much that we learned from each other. Anthony had the personality trait of someone that refused to be denied.

In 1994, I noticed that Anthony had a warrior mind-set. Anthony is the epitome of what a determined individual should be. A distinguished member of the air force, a college graduate, and a police officer, Anthony never let titles go to his head. He is probably the most humble human being I have ever had the pleasure of meeting. In January 1998, I saw Anthony patrolling the streets of Nashville for the first time. His boots were shined, uniform was clean, and badge was shining. I said to myself, "Dang! here is brother who looks good and will represent what our community needs to see day in and day out." *A strong black man.* I knew at that moment that once I finished college, I too would have my shot and would take advantage of every opportunity that comes my way. Anthony, Ken, and I studied hard every night meeting in the library and this paid dividends in our future development. All of us had one common goal in mind. We were determined to graduate from college and find our place in this world. Anthony had great study habits and all through college, he never made a grade lower than a B. I always reminded Anthony that not only was he my inspiration, but also my competition.

The Man That Has A Heart Of Gold

My friend Ken had several obstacles that he overcame after college, which ended up being lifelong learning lessons for both of us. A true measurement of a man's character is not when things are going good but during times of adversity. Ken is the type of brother that would give you the shirt off his back. Ken is very dependable, reliable, and honest. While in college, Ken was not an all A or B student. But, when it came to hard work and dedication, this man was second to none. I would put Ken's work ethic up against anyone and would be very confident that I got the best bet. You see, Ken didn't make the best grades, but he had the biggest heart. He had the heart of a giant. A lot of times, that's all you really need. The guy with the biggest heart will outshine the guy with the most smarts, any day.

Ken had a hard time seeking employment after college. It took Ken almost three years to get his breakthrough and land the job in the field that he had gone to school for. During this three-year-period of being underemployed, like many fresh college grads, frustration began to set in. You see, Ken was more dedicated to the process of finding a job than to the job itself. Because of his dedication to the process, Ken eventually found the perfect job for him. This process did not occur overnight, however, the timing was perfect. I have known Ken to fill out hundreds of applications and have things said to him like, "You're overqualified, so we can't pay you what you deserve." Or, "Come back in ninety days." Ken has gone through periods of unemployment and doors being slammed in his face; things that would discourage the average person. The beauty of it all was that nothing about Ken was really average. Ken once told me "When one door closes, God opens up another window. That window is called opportunity. When that window of opportunity opens up you need to seize the moment and jump through it."

A man needs to grab a hold of an opportunity the same way he does his lady. At times, an opportunity needs to be held, cherished, honored, and never forgotten in the same manner your lady does. Ken was very optimistic about his situation and never let the fact that others were talking about him get him down. This quality of his is what impressed me the most. How hard is it for a man to elevate to a higher level while being laughed at and ridiculed by his peers! It takes a strong man to overcome the status quo when he is on his way up, especially if the status quo says *stay where you are*. Ken knew where his faith and strength came from. Ken is a spiritual man, and I noticed that about him when we first met in 1994. Ken has demonstrated over the years that he is truly a dear friend, and it is a shame that the "golden globe determination award" can't be given to this man. It is too bad that one does not exist.

I want to leave you with the following message:

> *Be careful of your thought, for your thoughts become words.*
> *Be careful of your words, for your words become actions.*
> *Be careful of your actions, for your actions become habits.*
> *Be careful of your habits, for your habits become your character.*
> *Be careful of your character, for your character becomes your destiny.*

Author Unknown

Chapter 5

Don't Be A Victim

December 22, 1994, will forever be a memorable night the rest of my life. On this date, I became a victim of a violent crime. I had just completed my first semester of college, I was working part-time for UPS, my family was preparing for my father's retirement party in Chicago, and life was pretty good. It was standard policy that the university I was attending shut down during the winter breaks. The only people who remained on campus were athletes. Well, during this semester I was not an athlete, and I had to stay with a friend for a few weeks off-campus. My friend had an apartment in a North Nashville neighborhood that was known for violent crimes. I was fairly new to the city and did not know that I was going to be staying in a rough neighborhood.

I worked the midnight shift at UPS as a pre-loader as did several college students to earn a little extra income to assist with tuition. On this memorable night, I left my friend's apartment at about 12:30 a.m., en route to UPS. As I walked across the parking lot to my vehicle, I was approached by a black male, who was approximately five feet nine inches tall and 165 pounds and who came from a wooded area adjacent to the apartment complex.

As the man approached me, he said, "Hey, bro, you got a light?" I replied to him, "No, I don't smoke." The man got a little closer toward me. I knew as he started walking toward my vehicle that something was strange. As the man got closer, I looked into his eyes. I was able to tell that this man's eyeballs were bouncing around in his head. It was obvious that this individual was high on some type of controlled substance, possibly crack. I was able to see this even though it was pitch-black dark outside. It was also obvious from looking at this individual that he was running from someone or something.

He was dressed in ragged clothing and was sweating profusely. Before I knew it, the male subject closed the gap on me very fast, and he pulled out a black, semi automatic handgun and told me not to move. I paused for a moment and told the gunman, "Hey, brother, this is not necessary. What do you need?" The gunman replied, "Shut up and do what I say." Afraid of being shot, I complied with the verbal directives of the gunman. I was thinking to myself, *dang how could I let this guy get the drop on me?* I don't know if I was more upset at the fact that I was not really paying attention to my surroundings, or upset at the fact that I was being robbed at the hands of a man that had the same skin color as mine.

The male subject ordered me inside my vehicle. I got into the driver's side of my vehicle, and he got into the passenger side. With a gun in my side, I was ordered to start the vehicle and drive. I drove this man around town for about ten minutes. To say I was scared is an understatement. I had no idea where I was going. I knew that I had to do something, if I expected to survive this ordeal. I thought that this man was going to get me in an unfamiliar place where nobody would be able to find me. The thought of dying just days before Christmas just did not sit well with me. I was viewing the end of my life right before my eyes.

As frightening as that moment was for me, I quickly realized that there was a third person in the car with me. The third person was Jesus. Jesus was riding in the backseat of my vehicle and had control of the entire situation. With a gun pointed in my side and time working against me, I began to devise a plan in my mind. I was driving down a side street very slowly. I knew that if I continued to drive and got onto the main highway, I would have to drive at a higher speed, making my chances at a getaway slim to none. The plan was never to disarm the subject, but to get away from him as fast as I could. I knew the locks on my door were not secure, because I had power locks. I slowed the car down to about 30 mph. When I thought I had a decent chance to get away,

I opened the driver side door and jumped out the vehicle, while the car was still in motion. The male subject then slid over to the driver's side of my vehicle and sped off down the street.

I was surprised that I was not shot in the back or injured from my hard fall on the concrete. But like I said, Jesus was riding in the car with me the whole time. God's grace, His mercy, and my faith got me out of that situation alive. I managed to get away and run in the opposite direction, away from the gunman. I ran through the darkness and ran to the first house that had a porch-light on. I knocked on the door yelling and screaming, "Help, help, call 9-1-1." An elderly lady came to the door with a pistol in her hand and told me to get away from her door or she would shoot. I thought to myself, *is this not the epitome of someone who is really having a bad day?* I don't know anyone who has had two guns pulled on them in the same day just minutes apart from each other. There I was a true victim of a crime and a fellow citizen did not even want to help me.

I ran to another house and knocked on their front door as loud as I could. As luck would have it, I knocked on the door of an off-duty police officer. The officer answered the door and asked me what the problem was. I advised the officer that I had just been carjacked by a crackhead, and I needed police right away. The officer called for an on-duty patrol officer to respond to his home. Approximately fifteen minutes went by before the officer responded. When the officer arrived, that was the first sign of relief I had for at least thirty minutes. The officer that took my report was professional and understanding. She assured me that she would do everything within her power to catch the perpetrator. I gave the officer a statement of what had occurred and a report was made. The officer then gave me a ride to another friend's house where I phoned my parents in Chicago to let them know what had happened. If I could see the man that robbed me that night of my vehicle and all the contents that were inside, I would have no problem identifying him.

It's been over fifteen years since this ordeal occurred, and I have no ill feelings toward the man who robbed me. It did take some time for me to get over this traumatic situation. I feel that this was one of the experiences that have shaped me into the man that I am today. This may even be another contributing factor in my pursuing a career in law enforcement. It is truly a blessing, and it is only by God's grace that I am even around today to share this story. As I think back over the years, I have come to realize that not much has changed. There is still the issue of black-on-black crime. Black people are still the largest group represented on the lower end of the socioeconomic ladder, and black people are perceived even by our own people as a threat; therefore, making it harder for us to help our own people.

Just as I have been a victim of crime, I know some of you reading this book have been victims. Just because someone takes your property, don't allow them to take your soul. Use the fact that you have been victimized as motivation to strive to be the best you can be. Become an agent of social change and get over your fears. Please do not give someone that much power over your life. I know at times this may be a difficult task, but this is something you must do. We all have that inner strength to attack those that attack us.

The title of this chapter is "Don't Be A Victim." I realize that circumstances sometimes put you in situations that are beyond your control. What I challenge you to do, if you ever find yourself in a situation like this, is not to stop thinking. If you stop thinking, then you will stop living. Think about your family and your loved ones. These are the people who depend on you the most. What would you be willing to do if you knew someone was trying to permanently separate you from your family? Think about that for a moment? Don't ever feel like you have no way out. Keep your options open at all times. It's OK to be scared, but you need to remain steadfast in your inner confidence and faith in God. God puts us all through tests just to see where our faith is. But even more important, don't be a victim to economics circumstances and don't be a victim to lack of education. Too many people fall prey to these two entities which have long-term adverse effects on their ability to live productive lives and be positive contributors to society. Demand your place in this world and take advantage of both.

CHAPTER 6

Don't Listen to That Woman When She Says . . .

OK guys, if you are like most men, I'm sure you have heard women say that famous saying. Yeah, you know! The "I don't need a man saying." To my brothers out there, I'm here to tell you, don't' buy into that notion that some women are saying that they don't need a man. I am so happy to see that women are finally evening the playing field in corporate America. Furthermore, women are progressing in all aspects of life ranging from education, homeownership, and new businesses. Even though women are still making tremendous strides in the areas previously listed, especially minority women, they still lag far behind their male counterparts. With this said, the next time you hear a woman say that she does not need a man, don't you dare listen to that woman. She may not need you, but if she has your children your children will always need you. This is probably the only time I would recommend a man not to listen to a woman. Now in cases of abuse where there is physical and domestic violence taking place, all bets are off. No man has the right to put his hands on a woman unless it is in a loving and caring way. If a man does, then as far as I'm concerned it is probably in the best interest of the children—they don't see him a lot until the man gets some help in dealing with his aggressiveness. But, if you are a good man and you're not beating your woman or children, then you need to take a stand when it comes to those children. If both of you are single and no children are involved and the woman says she does not need you, that might be a good thing. This is the best time to break up. It does not matter how much in love you are. It does not matter how convenient it is to have each other around. The best time to cut ties in a relationship is before the children come. Just let her go ahead on her merry way. Most of the time this is the best for both of you in the long run.

Things become really complicated when a relationship goes south and there are children involved. If you don't believe me, check daily dockets at your local family court and look at all the divorce cases and child support cases pending. I personally think that before a couple gets married and contemplate having a family, they should go through some spiritual counseling with their pastor as well as go to a family court and listen to some of the cases that are brought before the court. This would be an eye-opening experience. I'm sure that people will take a more serious look at who they think they want to spend the rest of their lives with, let alone have a baby with. I bet this will cause people to ask the hard questions. Questions such as, *Do you want children or Do you have children from a previous relationship? What do you think is the most fundamental perspective in a marriage?* Questions like these almost never get asked on the front end of a relationship. If you want to see things get really complicated, try getting a divorce when children are involved. I believe that this process alone can age the average person five years. Think about this: What about the men that have three or four different women all of whom he has a child with out of wedlock? The issue of a man's character and integrity is in question when everywhere he goes he ends up leaving a baby behind. This is especially important for young men to understand. Take it from me, you are not defined a man based on the number of women you sleep with. A more accurate definition of a man can come from the number of women you are able to turn down and then deciding on the one you can be committed to. The bottom line is that women do need men just as much as men need women.

There are so many men out there that allow this "I don't need a man" stigma to prevent them from establishing and maintaining meaningful relationships with their children. As a result, over 50 percent of households in America are headed by single mothers. I think men downplay the importance of the role they play in their children's lives. This is especially the case when they are no longer in a relationship with the mother. As much as I am an advocate for meaningful relationships, I keep a realistic view that most relationships between men and women don't last. We have this inherent nature to want to change things after we have done the same thing over and over again. Relationships are no exceptions. It is hard trying to find a life partner to spend the rest of your days with. I wish more people would think about this before they decide to have children. You are forever linked to a person that you have a child with. There is no way around it.

When it comes to children, there are several types of men. I'm going to describe a few here for a moment. The first type of man is the one that won't do a damn thing! He can't be counted on, he is an absentee parent, and generally the type of person that does not need to have children around him, because the only thing he can teach them is what not to do. I know a young man from my old neighborhood that has nine children by seven different women. Of these nine children, six of them are boys. This young man has not married any of the women he has had a child by. This is a major problem that is all too common today. We are teaching our young men that it is socially acceptable to sleep around with as many women as they can and impreganant them thereby adversely impacting several lives at once bering no responsibility or consequences for their actions. This young man has never held down a steady job, nor, does he provide any type of support for his children. All of the women that he has had children by work trying to make ends meet. They are all single women and every day it is a struggle just to survive. How can a man like this be expected to teach young boys how to be men? I can't put all the blame on men. Women need to be a little more selective about who they have children with. Ladies, if you are dealing with a man who has children already that he does not take care of, what makes you think you can have a child with him and he will take care of your child? I know a lot of people don't want to hear this, but it has to be said. The same thing applies when a man is married and has a mistress on the side. Ladies, nine times out of ten *married men who cheat will not leave their wives for you!* Stop wasting your time and move on. For God's sake, don't have a baby by this man because the main person who will suffer is the child. The essence of what is being said is that ladies needs to be more selective in choosing their mate. Failure to choose the right mate could have dire consequences and impact more lives than you can ever imagine.

The second type of man is the one that continues to be an instrumental part of his child's life. This is the type of man that no matter what happens to the relationship between him and the mother, he will let nothing come in between the relationship he has established with the child. This type of man has decided this from the very beginning of his relationship with the mother. This type of man makes himself available at all costs. He does not attach a dollar value to his children. He understands that there is more to taking care a child than just sending a check once a month. He is fully committed to his duty as a man as well as a father. This type of man accepts the God-given challenge to teach his children right from wrong. He seeks out God for direction and wisdom. He is not afraid of making mistakes for he knows that through mistakes much is learned. This type of man takes pride in his children. His children in return look up to him. This type of man does not mind showing his feelings to his children. He understands that little boys and little girls need to understand that it is OK for a man to show he has feelings. Believe it or not, these are the type of men whom women respect and appreciate, even if they are no longer in a relationship together.

The third type is the man that wants to be involved, but allows the mother to dictate to him the terms and conditions of his involvement. Now this is where the court system comes in. Women use the system for their benefit, men must use the system for theirs. I believe that both parents who are responsible for bringing a child into this world should be able to come up with viable solutions together, on what the child needs and who will provide it without government intervention. The reality of the matter is more times than not, one party is usually acting on emotions that are not rational which is why so many cases end up in a family court. I believe of all the people involved in this process, the parents are the ones who have the best interest of the child at heart. At least that is what it should be. If you think the government is overly concerned with the welfare of your children, then you are sadly mistaken. The government just wants to make sure that children are not a burden on them. They couldn't care less whether a father spends quality time with his child as long as he sends the check every month. For God's sake, if you have children and you are breaking up, come up with something equitable between the two of you, and do not allow the government to tell you what you already know you need to do.

Most of the time, men don't want to spend the time, money, or energy on the front end to use the system to ensure court orders are equitable allowing them equal access to their children. Most men are content with the standard visitation of every other weekend and maybe two weeks out of the summer. *Whatever!* I am here to tell you guys, there is no way you can have any influence over your children's lives if you only see them twice a month and a few weeks during the summer. Now if you are a father and you live on the other side of the country far away from your children, and you are not willing to move closer so that your relationship with your children is not estranged, then yes, you have to pay and send money and other items to make sure your children have what they need. But, if you are in the same city or within a fifty-mile radius of your children, there is no reason for you to only make contact with them once or twice a month. If you are serious about raising your children, keeping them safe, ensuring they have access to health/medical services and a good education, then you will stop nothing short of joint custody to make sure this happens. Now I'm not attempting to give legal advice. I am attempting to challenge every man with children going through the family law system to exercise a little common sense. Fathers need to have just as much access to their children as the mothers do. The children need to know that. It is my opinion that in the minds of children, when they don't see Daddy much they get the feeling that his words are not worth the air that he breathes. Now we can't have that. Mommy and Daddy whether they are together or not, need to constantly be in the ears of their children and this in turn lets the children know that this is a tag team effort. There needs to be some sort of way that you are seeing your children daily or at the very least weekly to have an impact. A father's presence needs to be felt constantly. Daddy needs to make school visits to check on his children, Daddy needs to be the one doing homework sometimes with the kids, he needs to be available to talk to his children, to let them know that he loves and cherishes them, and he needs to remind his children that no matter what he will always be there for them. There should be no reason that you are able to see close friends or crackheads more than your own children.

I have the answer to why men agree to such orders in court. *Men are lazy . . .* Real men must actively be involved with their children's upbringing regardless of what the mother is saying. I think in the long run women respect men who make sure they will not be left out of the loop of their child's development. The family courts don't see this type of man very often. Men settle for a lot of things in life, but time with your children should not be one of them. If you and your soon-to-be ex don't work out, make sure the court order is something that you both can live with as well as something that will allow you to be a father to your children. You don't want to be in court every three to five years asking the court for a modification of child custody or child support. Get these issues squared away on the front end as early as you can. This is not the time to be lackadaisical. Believe me when I tell you, women are doing their homework when it comes to child custody and support so you better do yours as well. I'm not going to sugar coat this one bit. Child custody issues can run up a lengthy legal tab. I do think the ends justify the means. Can you really put a price tag on your children? It's worth it guys. Make it happen . . .

During a child custody issue, it is not the time to be liberal and be Mr. Nice Guy. "Men, you need to let the courts know that you are serious, the attorneys need to know that you are serious, and most of all if age is appropriate your children need to know that you are serious." As stated earlier, being a father involves much more than sending a check every month no matter how easy it may be. The family law system is set up to benefit the woman unless men challenges it in court. In order to challenge something in court, you need to be there. The problem is since most men don't challenge court orders, or even show up to the court, the court presumes the mother as the primary custodial parent and she gets whatever she wants. Maybe men think if they don't answer a subpoena or not show up in court, the issue will go away on its own. No, no no! Wrong answer. You will be held in *contempt*. Very often as men, we tuck our heads in between our legs and run off into the sunset because defeat has sat in our minds. Men think they don't have a chance in court to get joint custody or even full custody of their children because in past years, the children usually end up with the mother. News flash—more and more men have been getting custody of their children in the last twenty years. Gone are the days when men had no say in cases where their children are reared. Gone are the days when the only way a man got custody of his children was if the mother didn't want them or if there was something wrong with her. Courts have realized that men are just as capable of raising their children as women and more consideration is being placed on who actually would be the better parent. In no way am I giving legal advice. Contact a family attorney for that. What I am giving men is a common sense approach on how to deal effectively with the court system. As with anything else, before you take on an issue, you need to know your argument. That is what legal advisors and attorneys are for. But also, take time to invest in yourself. Acquire the knowledge you need to accomplish desired results. Don't just depend on someone to tell you what to do next. Be proactive and learn your rights as fathers. You owe that much to your children.

"Men, I'm here to tell you that you will lose 100 percent of the battles you never fight. Guys, don't be foolish. Fight to be fathers if that is what you have to do. Your children will one day have a profound respect for you when they grow up and find out that Daddy never left them behind and you were there with them every step of the way. Don't be taken advantage of and for God's sake don't be lazy. It takes much more than sending a check once a month to your children to have a meaningful impact on their lives. Men, you need to be there in the physical sense. Your presence is the key to your children's success." I wish there was a correlation between how much money a man sends his ex and the children, and the relationship he establishes with the children. The reality is that it's not. The court system is only concerned with the financial support of a child. They are not overly concerned with the quality time you spend or if you establish a bond with your child.

Chapter 7

Find Your Niche & Work It

Nothing is worse than going through life, just going through the motions. I don't care who you are, we all want to feel a part of something at some point in our lives. God did not place us here on earth among all the things that he created for us to function in isolation. There has to come a time in a man's life when he has to match up what he really likes doing with what he is actually good at. For some this can be a difficult task. For others it may be quite easy. It has been said that if you find something that you are passionate about then you never will work a day in your life. I truly believe that if you set your mind to do something that you are passionate about, you will figure out a way to sharpen your skills to become proficient.

My sister Jacquelyn Digby-Allen has a military background. She was always focused on what she needed to do and never let anything pull her off task. She kept me on task while I was a college student. She reminded me on a weekly basis that pain was temporary and pride was forever. I took the words that she said to heart then and I still do today. I remember going to her graduation at Parris Island, South Carolina, in 1989. On a hot summer day, my sister became a United States Marine. She stood tall and firm with a look of confidence displayed across her face. I was proud, she was proud, and our entire family was proud. I learned at that moment that the sky was the limit. I knew that the only person that was going to stop me from accomplishing my goals was me. My sister Jacquelyn was approximately 115 lbs when she went through basic training. I thought to myself, "How could someone so small accomplish something so big?" Since serving her country with pride, Jacquelyn has attained her undergraduate and graduate degrees and she is a distinguished professional in the Allied Health field. This was a major motivational factor for me in my pursuit to find my niche and my purpose.

The former head coach of the Indianapolis Colts, Tony Dungy, comes to mind when I think of a man who has a true balance of being a father, a man, and being a success. Coach Dungy has written two books that are must-reads for any man striving to acquire a good balance in life. His teachings have assisted me a great deal and his school of thought is unique in nature. In his books *Uncommon* and *Quiet Strength*, Coach Dungy talks about success from a societal standpoint and the notoriety that comes from being in the public eye. Professional excellence, fame, and celebrity status are great; however, Coach Dungy stressed that through all the highs and lows of winning championships and overcoming obstacles on the football field, this has had very little to do with his ultimate significance as a man. A leader, father, author, and role model, Coach Dungy challenges each of us as men to take an inside look at our lives and to start to really focus on things that matter.

I know a lot of people who are good at a job they hate going to everyday. And then there are those people who love what they do but are not that good at doing it. These type of people never quite get to the point in their lives where the gift that they have been given has revealed itself to them. Booker T. Washington, in *Up from Slavery*, said, "Cast down your buckets where you are." In essence, Washington was saying don't ask for too much too fast. Be patient and work hard in the present because the future is going to bring greater things. If you are a ditch digger today, then you be the best ditch digger you can be. Stop worrying about what other people are saying. Don't ask for things that if you get, you won't be able to handle it anyway. No matter what your job is, have pride in it until something better comes along.

I have always believed that some of the best basketball players are not in the NBA. I believe some of the best athletes are not on the professional level at all. I believe that the best basketball players can be found on any given day on the basketball courts in every city across America. These young men play just for the love of the game. These are the brothers who never used their God-given talent to take them beyond the boundaries of their neighborhoods. What a shame. I know an eighteen-year-old kid who can kick a football fifty plus yards consistently. He can be found standing at the corner store drinking beer and smoking marijuana with the other homeboys. Oh, and by the way, he is a high school dropout. Does this sound familiar? Nothing should bother you more than to wake up everyday and look at all the wasted talent that is around you.

What's the difference between Michael Jordan and the streetball player? Both have talent and they both have a passion for the game of basketball. Both could easily play on the same level and have the same amount of success. The real difference is that Michael Jordan made some smart choices along the way and the baller on the streets didn't. It's as simple as that. Michael Jordan used basketball to pay for his college education. The streetball player thinks he is going to get educated by playing basketball. Many people don't know that Michael Jordan was cut from his high school basketball team. His coach at the time thought that he was not good enough. Michael Jordan with that burning competitive spirit knew his destiny and what layed ahead. Michael Jordan refused to be denied. He found his niche and started developing it at an early age. The end result was a man who went on to become a success at the college and the professional levels, reaching the highest honor possible in the world of sports which was winning a goal medal in Barcelona in 1992. To say this man was a hard worker is an understatement. You see, a dream delayed is not a dream denied. The next time somebody tells you what you can't do, you remind them of what God can do. If you have God-given talent to do something, there is nothing anybody can do to stop you, except yourself. You are your own worst enemy. Let people who attempt to discourage you know that you serve on a higher level to a higher power.

Don't Underestimate The Power Of An HBCU

I attended Grambling State University in Grambling, Louisiana, for a brief period before transferring to Tennessee State University, in Nashville,

Tennessee. Both of these institutions provided me with similar experiences. I saw strong, powerful, and educated black men who had lived distinguished lives and were willing to mentor me to do the same. All they asked in return for their service was that I allow myself to be taught and I kept a good attitude. I must give credit to where credit is due. Grambling State and Tennessee State are both historically black universities with long track records of producing excellence. This is the goal of all historically black colleges and universities—to give the black man an extra sense of belonging and purpose. An education from an HBCU allowed me to question the unknown and challenge the unheard. It was there that I was nurtured and groomed by the best. Most of my professors while in college were black men. My father had given me a foundation which I was able to build on by attending these universities. My male professors were nothing more than an extension of my father. The only difference was that my dad lacked the formal education of these men. My female professors were nothing short of being my mother. Prof. L. B. Gaiters from the Department of Criminal Justice at Tennessee State University checked up on me just as a mother checks up on her children. Professor Gaiters made sure that I did not forget the real reason I was attending college in the first place—to get an education. The point is that the education from these institutions has proven to be some of the best you can get anywhere in the United States. I am proud that these institutions helped me develop as a man and as a productive member of society. I now have a purpose beyond what I even thought existed when I started out on my college journey in 1994.

    The key is figuring out early what you are good at, to give yourself time to maximize your potential. Now I do not want to imply that if you figure out your niche later on in life it is a bad thing. I do want you to understand that the earlier you take control of your life as a young adult, the longer amount of time you may have to enjoy what you do and help the next person. It's just like saving for a rainy day. If you save for a long period of time while times are good, when things get bad you won't be affected much because you will be prepared. It's just like that old saying, "It's better to have a hundred dollar bill and not need it, than to need it and not have it." Just food for thought. Not all of us can be a professional athlete. But, I challenge each one of you reading this book to try to develop an athlete's work ethic. Whatever it is that you're good at; I want you to try putting in the same amount of hours working on it that an athlete spends on the football field or the basketball court. I guarantee that you will become very proficient in that area over time. I realize that it takes some people longer to find out just what they are good at than other people. It is important to understand that this process should be never ending. In the Bible it states that no man is perfect except Jesus Christ Himself. But, that should not stop you from striving to be perfect and becoming a success in God's eyes. You should never get to the point where you lack the desire to continue to learn. To dream is a beautiful thing. Whether you realize it or not, when you're dreaming you are actually thinking. Thoughts are things. The thought of what could be or what might be, should always race through the minds of the young and old. What I hate to hear people say when they get older is, *"I wish I had done that, If only I had known, If I could turn back the hands of time, or I never had the opportunity."* These are all indicative of people who have regrets in later years because they failed to be proactive in their career development and growth as individuals. It is never too late to strive to better yourself.

You don't want to be one of those men at sixty-years old talking about what you should have done when you were twenty-five, having big time regrets about your life. Hindsight is 20/20. It is easy to say today what you could have done yesterday. However, we all need to get to the point where when we get older we are saying to ourselves, *"I'm glad I did what I did twenty-five years ago because I would not be where I am today if I had not done what I did."* As stated in earlier chapters, the life you live will be a direct result of the decisions you make. You are the architect of your own design. The foolish-minded individuals will do nothing. They will sit back and take what is given to them. They will never find their purpose in life because they are waiting for someone else to find it for them. If you allow someone else to discover your purpose, believe me when I tell you that they probably won't share it. Instead, you will become a little fish in a big pond just waiting to be eaten alive by a shark. The smart people will realize their self-worth early. They begin to put things into action early enough to where even if it does not go as planned and they fail, they actually take away with them the learning experience of the matter. Smart-minded people will not count pennies today, they will count dollars earned tomorrow. They realize that tomorrow is vastly approaching and they want to acquire the knowledge, skills, and abilities of tomorrow, and not today. They are fully aware of the fact that skills learned today will be obsolete in five years, unless those skills are built upon a foundation of continuing education. These type of individuals understand that the path to their ultimate success begins and ends with them. They leave nothing to chance.

They understand that leadership principles not only applies to how well they lead their professional lives but their personal lives as well. They are determined to turn nothing into something. They constantly aspire to set new goals and objectives, and they realize that their ultimate success occurs not by becoming successful themselves, but by assisting those around them to reach their highest potential levels, therefore, defining their success. Self-motivation and initiative are second nature.

When I was younger, I would often go to the basketball courts and play basketball with the best of them. As a teenager, I played basketball, baseball, and ran track with guys who are now on the professional level in their respective sports. I remember guys like Reginald Hayward and Donovan McNabb who both played football from my old neighborhood. These guys are now professional athletes. I grew up with these guys and watched them develop over the years. They did not evolve into the men they are today overnight. As boys, both guys found their niche at an early age. I believe they both were about eight years old when they began playing football. Hard work and dedication for these guys began when most kids at their age were busy running around, playing video games, and wasting time. Their parents were visionaries and helped them develop their niche early. The end result being two great athletes.

When I played basketball as a teen, I thought that I was better than average. This is, however, just my opinion. I witnessed firsthand some guys I knew that could have played on a professional level. When I played, I never considered trying to take it to a higher level. I had other goals and aspirations

"Why You Need To Be The Man"

I wanted to go after. In my junior year at Thornwood High School, my track coach Gary Haupert saw that I had talent that would benefit the track team and he recruited me. This was a life changing event for me. For someone to notice the potential that I did not even know I had was truly a blessing. Coach Haupert brought out that potential in me. Coach Haupert taught me that competitive nature and teamwork go hand in hand. In doing so, he also reinforced the student athlete concept. I learned that before we traveled anywhere for a track meet that I was representing my school as a student who happened to be an athlete. This was not something taken lightly. Coach Haupert did not do this alone and had the support of the staff, faculty, and school district.

I had several teachers who took an interest in my academic as well as athletic achievements. My teammates Reginald Torian, Jason Easterly, Herb Washington, Charles Juniors, and a list of other teammates held me accountable and constantly let me know that if greatness is what I was seeking, then I must be willing to do what my competitors were not willing to do. *Practice, Practice, Practice* and when you get finished, *practice some more.* I was fortunate to attend a high school where the talents of students were recognized inside and outside the classroom by faculty and staff, as well as other students. I can remember weekly grade sheets that went around to all of the athletes' teachers in the school. These sheets were turned in every week. If a student was doing below average in any class during the week, he/she was unable to participate in the following week's game or competition in their respective sports. I loved my teammates, loved my school, and most of all loved my community. I did not ever want to do anything that jeopardized my ability to compete because of my inability to perform in the classroom. The same people who were watching me were the same people who were supporting and encouraging me. I was held accountable to my community, my school, my parents, my teammates, and I'm sure to many other people whom I never met.

When you develop your niche, it involves you being at a certain point in your life. Development occurs at different stages. In high school, my track coach, team members, teachers, and staff helped me develop the niche of self-confidence and team work. This allowed me to get through high school and stay focused on the things that were important. As I mastered self-confidence and team work, I was prepared to enter the next phase of my life that I would undertake in college. In my senior year of high school, the self-confidence really kicked in. I realized that the only person that was going to stop me from going to college and furthering my education was me. I also realized that God put other people on this earth around me to learn from. I understood that just as others could be a blessing to me, I must also be a blessing to them. It is a beautiful thing to have people around you to help support you with accomplishing your goals and aspirations. What has bothered me as I have gotten older is the number of young men I see not maximizing their potential. There is very little goal setting, there is no finding your niche, and for many of these young men there is no future.

The Back Breaking Work

In chapter 5, I talked briefly about my tenure at UPS. I worked for UPS during the seasonal peak periods of the year. This was usually the months from October through January. UPS had an excellent working relationship with the local colleges and universities offering part-time work to financially strapped students, to help offset tuition cost. If you had done a good job and there was room available, management would evaluate you and determine whether or not they should hire you on as a full-time employee and work throughout the year. During this peak period, this was not the time to call off or be written up. This did not put you in a very favorable light with management. I never wanted to work for UPS throughout the year. The hours were very convenient for me during the holiday season and the pay was not too bad for a college student. The pay was somewhere around ten dollars per hour and I would work five hours shifts. Ten dollars per hour for a college student was good money in 1994. I worked in the pre-load department for a few months. The people who were assigned to the pre-load were the ones who loaded the little brown trucks that delivered small packages to homes all across America. I can remember being assigned five trucks with each truck having approximately thirty zip codes a piece that I had to remember. Packages were placed in cages on a conveyor belt and each pre-loader was assigned a cage color. My cage color was red which meant that as the red cage came around on the conveyor belt, I was responsible for pulling as many packages from the red cage as I could and placing it on the correct truck.

Anyone that has worked for UPS knows that it is extremely hard work. If you're not in shape and you go and work for UPS, after about three weeks you will be in excellent shape. It was an ongoing process that I thought would never end. Management would constantly walk up and down the line yelling, "Let's move it people, let's move it, we got get these packages out the cages, let's go, let's go. You're getting paid good money up in here, let's do it, do it." I was nineteen years old at the time and I thought I could take on the world. I was motivated and excited to be part of a team. My team got the packages out of the cages and onto the back of those trucks where they were delivered in the same day. I knew that if I failed to do my job and not get the packages on the trucks they were supposed to be on, the company would lose money. If the company lost money because of my error, I lost credibility with the management. This was the working personality of the hub. Every pre-loader was held accountable for a package that ended up going to the wrong place. For five long hours I worked pulling packages from the cages until my cages were all empty. It was only then I was able to go home and my shift was officially over. Going home though was only a thought. Often times, when I finished loading the little brown trucks with the small packages, I would work another shift as a driver helper for overtime. At UPS we got overtime everyday if we worked more than the required five hours. For me, that meant my overtime rate was fifteen dollars per hour. Again, this was not bad money for a struggling college student. A driver helper would ride out with the drivers at 6:00 a.m. in the morning delivering the packages to local businesses on their routes. The helper would be out on a route with a driver for another five hours if they wanted to. This money came in real handy around Christmas time. Every driver in the hub had an assigned route and almost all drivers wanted a driver helper. A helper meant that the driver would never have to get off the truck to make a delivery. All the driver did was drive. The helper was the one who got off the truck to deliver the packages and get the necessary signatures.

There was anywhere from fifteen to twenty stops on a route. If the route was in a rural area, sometimes this required a lot of excessive walking, often times in inclement weather. This was hard work, but rewarding to say the least. You probably will not find too many overweight UPS drivers with all the on the go moving they have to do.

When the weekends came, you can believe that I appreciated every minute of it. Working a job like this did several things. The first thing it did was kept me out of trouble. Even if I had been a troublesome kid, I was often too tired to do much more than go to class and then to sleep. Secondly, as great a job as this was, I learned that this was not something that I wanted to do the rest of my working years. Working for UPS was just one more reason I decided to continue my education to do something different. My theory was to work smart not work hard. And to say that I was working hard at UPS is an understatement. The third thing I learned was the value of hard work. I viewed working at UPS as the rite of passage. I had to pay my dues. I needed to experience what hard work was all about. I needed to sweat and get my hands dirty. UPS created a value system in me that I continue to carry with me to this day. I am so grateful that I had the opportunity to experience manual labor at the age of nineteen. I was working next to adult men and women who encouraged me to stay in school and make a better life for myself. These men and women were breaking their backs everyday just to make ends meet.

Just when I thought working in the pre-load department of UPS was hard work, I thought the grass was greener on the other side. I transferred to the unload/loading department. In this department, I was responsible for loading and unloading eighteen wheeler UPS truck. I promise you when I say it was ninety degrees outside, it felt like 190 degrees inside one of those truck trailers. I lost twenty pounds in my first month in this new department. My father always told me a little hard work never hurt anybody.

Can you imagine working thirty years in a field that you hate? What about working in a field that you are not being properly trained for? Do you think this will have an impact on your self-worth? Do you think your value with a company will decrease or increase if you fail to keep up-to-date with the latest techniques? These are just a few questions that you need to ask yourself as you go through the daily grind of your nine to five shift. If you are like most people, you work anywhere from forty to fifty hours a week. This is a lot of hours to spend somewhere that you dread going. There are three areas in life that a person should remain happy in. These areas are career, relationships, and everything else. The Lord has been too good to all of us and there is absolutely no reason why any of us should go through life unhappily. Statistics say that we will switch careers five to six times in our working career. This is a drastic change from the way things once were. In the early to mid part of the twentieth century, men found jobs in manufacturing and the auto industry that they worked for thirty to forty years. In today's society, the average man works on a job less than five years and then he switches to another job. In order to be successful in all your endeavors, it is important that you establish two things. These things are: 1) a plan, and 2) a vision.

A Plan

In the process of finding your niche, you need to begin with a plan. Included in this plan should be time lines. Also included in your plan should be an accountability factor. You need to always hold yourself to a standard that nobody holds you to or knows about. This is a means of keeping yourself in check. A plan does not have to be written to scale; however, some ideas need to be concrete and realistic. A plan keeps you thinking. It keeps the wheels in your brain turning. Constant planning keeps you sharp and ready for the unexpected. Of course, you don't want to be an excessive planner. You don't want to overindulge in anything. You need to remember one thing as stated earlier; if you fail to plan you may as well plan on failing. This is the case whether you are a high school student, a college student, a CEO of a major company, a manager, or anyone else. A plan is nothing more than a blueprint or a road map to get to where you want to be. I realize that some things are great when done on the spur of the moment. This can be quite exciting. For example, a surprise night out with your significant other, or a surprise dinner. Or maybe even a little two-to-three day getaway just to break away and have some time to yourself. We all need this from time to time. But there are things that need to be carefully thought out and planned. Some of these things include your education, your financial future, when to marry, when to have children, career choices, where to worship, etc. I believe that you cannot wait until you become a father before you plan on being a good one. If you plan on being a good father, there are several things that you need to be working on while you are still single. For example, being responsible, hard working, being patient, being committed, showing your unselfishness, and most of all being flexible. Every great idea starts with a plan.

A Vision

A vision is just an extension of your plan. A person who has vision has power. A vision allows you to look beyond your current situation and make a projection as far as fifteen to twenty years into the future. A visionary will make it through the storm no matter how bad things may appear. Visionaries have wisdom. They are smart enough to not let their current situation dictate their future paths. Visionaries anticipate some stumbling blocks in the road. A visionary plans for the worse possible outcome. If the worse possible outcome occurs, it is not an emergency to a visionary. If the worse possible outcome never occurs then he has not lost anything. As many of you know, the stock market hit rock bottom in 2009. Many people's lifesavings were wiped out. As a result, this caused many people to change their investment portfolio. People who were short-term planners panicked and took their money out of the stock markets and were taxed heavily. Now, I want to be clear, this book is not about financial planning, nor, am I a financial adviser. I am however, a visionary in that my investment strategies are not short term. They are long term in nature. A person who is a visionary is not concerned with the stock market hitting rock bottom because as part of their overall plan, they realize that the volatility of the stock market is just a redistribution of wealth. They know that every twenty or so years, the stock market takes a nosedive only to come back hard. A visionary's goal should be to invest in projects and programs that will outlive him/her. Look at the following table.

Plan	Vision
Short term: 0-5 years	Long term: 10 years and beyond
Not concrete	Focused intense
Very few people are involved	Many are involved
Initially has little impact on others	Impacts many people in the future. For example: future generations

When I was in college, I was just like all the rest of the students. I wanted to pursue a career in my field when I graduated. Who really wants to go to college for four years only to find out that when you get finished you can't get a job? That would be a tough pill to swallow for anyone. Let me be frank if I may. If you think for one minute that all you have to do to ensure your success is go to college and earn a four year degree, I have some bad news. Get your head out of the sandbox. You are living in a fantasy world. The real education begins when you finish college. The first lesson you will learn is that you probably won't get what you think you deserve in the first attempt. The world has this strange way of smacking people in the face who think they deserve something, just because they have a piece of paper in their hand that says bachelor's degree. Part of education is understanding the world we live in and being able to adapt to any given situation you may find yourself in. College in and of itself does not guarantee success. If you mix that college education with determination, motivation, work experience, and drive, and occasionally a little luck then and only then can you take advantage of what wonderful things higher education can provide. A college degree is the extra topping on an already made up dessert. A big part of education is to understand the process of continuing to educate yourself long after you acquire those certifications and degrees. Putting yourself in a situation that will allow you an advantage over those individuals who lack the necessary traits to become successful is the essence of finding your niche.

Get out of that age-old habit of just working a job without a plan. There is nothing wrong with working a job, but people must learn how to make a job work for them. You have to understand that there are plenty of jobs out there in the world to choose from. What your sights should be focused on is what career you want to go after. Working a particular job can prepare you for a particular career. From 1996 to 1999, I was employed with a company named Guardsmark Inc. There could not have been any better job for me at that time. When I speak of finding your niche, I'm also talking about doing what you have to now so that you can do what you want to later. Working at Guardsmark Inc. allowed me to attend college during the day, while working security at night. Guardsmark gave me the opportunity to gain valuable experience in the security industry while earning my criminal justice degree. I worked for this company at the same time this company worked for me. I showed them that I was responsible, honest, and dedicated and in return they made sure my shifts were flexible and I worked the hours that I wanted. This was a great trade-off. Little did I know that once I finished college, Guardsmark would offer me the opportunity to go into their manager training program. This was the company's way of saying to me that they valued my service and commitment. I took the time to further my education and as a result, they wanted to give me more responsibility, training, and pay.

    A good indicator for anyone who is looking for a company to work for while attending college at the same time is if that company promotes education. I mean really promote education. What I mean by promoting education is by ensuring that you have a flexible work schedule allowing you to attend college classes. Another way companies can promote education is by providing education incentives for employees who set and maintain certain grade point averages. Employee growth and development from within is a big plus. This is really big because nothing is as rewarding as working for a company that decides to promote you within the company, after you have demonstrated your commitment level to furthering your education and making your company a more desirable place to work. A company that allows you to put into practical perspective what you are going to school for should also rise to the top of your list as a potential place of employment while you are pursuing your college degree. For instance, if you are pursuing a business degree and the company you are working for or seeking to work for allows you to work in an area that broadens your knowledge in areas like accounting or accounts payable. This will give you firsthand experience in your field of study that you can talk about when you start interviewing for career jobs. Don't be afraid of starting at the bottom of any organization as long as you don't plan to stay there. Now if you don't continue to educate yourself and take on new challenges to demonstrate your proficiency level, then don't plan on moving up too soon. You may as well plan on staying right where you are, making the same money as more time goes by, and staying in a position where you don't have many choices. As a matter of fact, you may need to get ready to move out of that position either by termination or resignation because if you're not showing your net worth to your employer, they will find someone who will—the end result being not able to provide for your family adequately, feeling less of a man, getting older, and having a bad attitude. Now I know this is pretty harsh, but it is something that needs to be emphasized. Knowledge is power.

Our country is currently in the middle of one of the worst recessions in U.S. history. There are many people out of work. If you are fortunate enough to have a job or a career for that matter in 2010, you need to be smart enough to keep it. It may not be the best job, but make it work for you until you better your position to move on. It is very foolish to quit a job and you don't already have something else lined up. For God's sake, don't you ever do this. I don't care how bad the job is or how bad you hate your boss. Have the self-discipline to stick it out. There have been people who have started at the bottom of an organization and worked their way all the way to the top. The benefit of doing this is you learn firsthand the duties and responsibilities of each level as you progress upward through the organization. The end result being a more well-rounded quality individual.

One problem I see with the younger generation is that they want to experience instant gratification. Think about how we live our lives today. We live in the age of the Internet, MySpace, Facebook, Twitter, PlayStation, credit cards, and many other instruments that allow us to do and get what we want instantly. Technology is great, but it does come at a great cost. Think for a moment about your cell phone. I know that there may be a few people who still don't have cell phones but most people do. Think about the telephone numbers in your contact list. How many of them do you know by memory? I am a betting man, and I believe that most people probably can't recall by memory two numbers out of their contact list because technology has fixed it to where all you need to do is press a button. It is so convenient and convenience is what has gotten us stupid. We no longer train the mind to commit things to memory. Think about the days before cell phones. You committed everybody's telephone number to memory that you talked to on a regular basis. This is because you forced your mind to work. Technology has worked for us and it has worked against us. Technology has caused a lot of people to become lazy. Technology has also caused a disconnect among our young people in their ability to use their social interaction skills. Young people today experience difficulty in communicating orally in the language of business as well as day to day social communication in the home and school. The reason being is that they simply are not required to anymore. Technology has made it possible to now communicate through electronic devices without ever opening your mouth or making eye contact. We must all recognize the limitations that technology is placing on our young people and get back to the basics. Technology companies are making millions of dollars to keep our children stupid. Keep this in mind the next time you go to the store to buy your child a gadget that will diminish his/her ability to effectively communicate orally and in writing.

It amazes me when I talk to young people and older people who tell me that they want a fifty thousand dollars a year job, but don't want to go through any formalized training to put them in a position to make that happen. They want to make this big money, but higher education is nowhere in the plan. Where do we get off passing this entitlement logic on to our children? We have a generation of young people who believe that money grows on trees and they don't have to shake the tree hard for the money to fall. I believe that some people actually think if they just keep living long enough doing the bare minimum, somehow good things are just going to happen for them. Or maybe these groups of people feel that if they just keep living, somebody who has worked hard and did their due diligence will just give them a leg up or a spring board to a life of progress and success. *Wrong, Wrong, Wrong!* In most cases, instant gratification is not really good. Instant gratification only gives people a false sense of security into believing that everything in life comes easy when in actuality that is not the case. Anything in life that is worth having is worth working for.

Any time a person gets too much too fast they become overwhelmed. You can always tell when a person is not accustom to something. When a person is not accustom to something, they act on impulse. This means that they act without thinking about the possible consequences of their actions. They don't know what to do. I believe that anything that a person wants more of, they need to figure out a way to give more of that same thing. For example, if you want more money, then you need to give more money. If it is more time that you want for yourself or your family, then you need to figure out a way to give more of your time. We have all heard stories of people who go from rags to riches and then right back to rags in a short period of time. Good examples of this are the people who win millions of dollars with state lotto's. I have heard all too often that many of these people have gone through all their money in a relatively short period of time. How does a person go through twenty million dollars and not have anything to show for it? Well, the answer is improper training, lack of knowledge, and lack of discipline. There is an old saying that "Money just enhances who you really are." If you were a crackhead without money, no large amount of money will cure you from your crack habit. If you come across a large sum of money, you will now just be a crackhead with money. I'm sure you will be able to buy more of it. If you were a kindhearted and giving person, money will just intensify this characteristic. We are all creatures of habit. If a person is not accustom to having something and all of a sudden they obtain it quickly, they usually end up losing it as fast as they got it. Furthermore, people who acquire things that they did not have to work for usually do not appreciate the value of the asset anyway. This is the case whether it is money, a job, relationship, or any other tangible item.

A Career of Excellence

For a lot of people, the main reason they find it difficult to really explore what they are good at comes right down to effective leadership. Effective leadership differs from effective management. Effective leadership comes down to doing what's right because it is the right thing to do. Effective management comes down to making the most popular decision whether it is the right thing to do or not. They both are important, but I think leadership at the end of the day wins the battle.

My current supervisor Sgt. Lloyd Brown is one individual who I can truly say demonstrates true leadership abilities. I say that because Sergeant Brown is a person who can recognize the hidden talents of individuals he supervises. A true leader can bring out the best in the people working for him/her. A true leader can recognize the hidden talents in individuals that the individuals themselves don't even know they have. A true leader does not mind taking chances when the time is right as well as giving other people chances. Sergeant Brown gave me an opportunity to explore some hidden talents of mine. He did this by allowing me the chance to specialize in an investigative capacity. True leaders don't mind going against the status quo. True leaders know that at some point they must challenge their troops. True leadership understands that once you assume a leadership role it is no longer about you. Your success as a leader is then contingent upon the success of those you help succeed. This is what Sergeant Brown has done for many who have worked for him. He has helped them find their niche. Sergeant Brown has armed himself with the knowledge, skills, and abilities to succeed as a leader. He has reached a point in his career to where he wants to pass on the knowledge that has taken him over twenty-five years to gain. A true leader realizes that he may not see his vision completed and because he may not see it, he tries to educate those coming behind him to carry on the torch. In 1999, Fred Manske wrote a book titled, *Secrets of Effective Leadership.* He stated, "Leaders are needed to light the way to the future and to inspire people to achieve excellence. Furthermore, to be an effective leader the idea is to slowly build everyone's confidence—to develop the attitude of being a winner."

Chapter 8

Know Where Your Strength Comes From

It's a beautiful Sunday morning on this Easter of 2010. God has blessed me yet again to celebrate another year. I look at all the children in their Sunday's best. Little boys and little girls are excited. Many of them know that after Sunday morning service they would feast somewhere and then the big Easter egg hunt would be under way.

I love Easter because it is just another reminder to me of why I'm still here. It is another reminder of just how great our God really is. It should also be another reminder to you of why you are still here also. Pastor Kenneth Robinson and Marilyn Robinson are co-pastors at St. Andrew AME, in Memphis, Tennessee. AME stands for African Methodist Episcopal. I have never in my life seen such a wonderful tag team approach at delivering God's word. These two leaders are the epitomes of what a husband and wife can accomplish together if God is the head of the relationship.

I started attending St. Andrew AME in 2005, at the request of my fiancé, Jacqueline Elaine Nunley. Today, Jacqueline and I are married. Every chance I get I head to Memphis to attend St. Andrew AME to hear God's word. I already had a connection to the AME church in Dallas, Texas. It was in Dallas, I began attending St. Paul AME, in 2003. I have since felt a spiritual connection with the AME church. It is for this reason, I continue to go and fellowship every week and I support their teachings. Since I became affiliated with the AME church, God has been moving ever so powerfully in my life. It seemed as if everything just started to fall in place. In 2003, I felt for the first time that my life was striking a balance. I believe that everything happens for a reason and I am in my rightful place.

It was ironic that Pastor Juan Tolliver of St. Paul AME, in Dallas knew Pastor Robinson at St. Andrew AME, in Memphis personally. These two men loved me enough to get together and encouraged me to attend St. Paul on a full-time basis. Dallas is where I live and is where I consider home. Both of these extraordinary men agreed that I needed to fellowship on a full-time basis where I resided. As a result, Pastor Tolliver has put me under watch care for as long as I am a resident of North Texas. Both of these men have embraced me and I truly feel like I am connected to an extended family.

As Pastor Kenneth Robinson was delivering his Easter Sunday message to the congregation, I sat there with my family and listened attentively. I could not stop thinking about what Jesus had to go through in order for me to live today. I thought to myself, what type of man could endure that type of pain and still have love for those who persecuted Him? I thought wow, what a horrible way to die. Being nailed to a cross, being hit, being spit on, being stoned, I could not even imagine what else. Pastor Robinson spoke on the fears that prevent God's people from prospering and seeking out their purpose. He related this to the fears that Jesus must have had as he was being tortured and crucified. Pastor Robinson went on to say through all the fears that Jesus must have had, he did not disobey God. Men must do the same thing. We cannot disobey God when we have been given spiritual instructions.

It was a very powerful message and one that hit right home for me. Each and every time I visit St. Andrew AME, I can feel the power of God moving through the entire building. In order for me to live today, Jesus had to die. Jesus is the insurance policy and all of us are the beneficiaries. Isn't it amazing that when you talk to some people they all say they want to go to heaven but nobody wants to die. I continued to think about the real significance of Easter.

What has bothered me more over the years is the number of children who do not understand the significance of Easter in the first place.

Easter is not about hunting Easter eggs, eating the best meal of your life in one day, or looking better than you have all year. Easter is about realizing that Jesus made the ultimate sacrifice for all of us by laying his life down and three days later rising up again. More importantly, Jesus was guided by His faith and not fears to accomplish God's will. Where does your strength come from? Do you think you have the strength to take on life's challenges? Life is the biggest challenge all of us must fight. If the proper strategy is used, you can place yourself on equal playing ground with life and the fight won't be so bad. This is not to say it will be easy. Indeed obstacles and roadblocks will be thrown your way. The point is having that inner strength that can only come from a higher power to see you through.

Just like anyone else, I have personal problems that I need advice in handling. Don't ever get to the point where you think you don't have to listen to anyone. At the same time, don't believe everything that people tell you. Go the extra mile and seek second opinions if you need to. Have you ever gone to a doctor and found that the doctor always had the answer to your problem? You might think this is good. I would become very concerned. I get concerned because anyone who has all the answers to everything is probably only right 20 percent of the time. Sometimes it's OK to say "I don't know." The only person who has all the answers to your problems is the Almighty God Himself....

It is not uncommon at all to find people who always seem to have all the answer to your problems to have mega problems of their own. It is very difficult for people who are in positions of control to relinquish that control to someone else. The fear of their true identity will be exposed and for many in positions of power this is intolerable.

Dan Pride has been a great friend of mine for the last fifteen years. Our friendship goes back to our college days; however, in 2003, I saw a side of Dan Pride I had never seen. In 2003, I found out that Dan had become an ordained minister. Rev. Dan Pride is responsible for assisting me acknowledge many of my shortcomings. I have confided in him personal matters and God has worked through him to give me sound advice. I have called Reverend Pride by phone in the middle of the night to talk with him on issues that were heavy on my heart. Reverend Pride knew exactly what to say to calm the situation and most importantly reminded me that the problems I had were nothing new. He reiterated to me the problems I had were the same problems he had and were just problems of the world. He challenged me to never forget that everything works for the good of God no matter how bad we think the situation is. Reverend Pride is the youth minister at St. Paul AME and connects really well with the youths in the church. This is what impressed me the most with Reverend Pride. In college, he was a leader on the football field. Today he uses his leadership skills to make a difference in the lives of God's children.

Men have the tendency to think the more weights they lift or the harder they train, the stronger they become. This may be true in its physical sense. What I'm talking about is a different type of strength. I'm talking about the strength that is developed inside a man. I'm talking about the strength that is developed from a higher power. Real men know and understand that they can only move mountains with the help of the Lord. Have you ever been in a situation where you could not see yourself out? Have you ever felt like everybody has turned their backs on you and you were left in the cold? What did you do? How did this make you feel? When all else fail, where do you turn to for help? These are some hard questions that many people have no answer to.

From Corporate to Convict

My friend, Terry, was on top of the world. He had a whopping six figure salary of $220,000 per year. At the age of thirty-seven he thought things were going pretty well. He was a success in his career, had a wonderful family, had a beautiful home, and the future was looking very bright. Then all at once his world came crashing down. First, he was laid off his six figure job. He reported to work at 8:00 a.m. on a Tuesday and when he sat down at his desk, he had a pink slip that read *due to company downsizing your position has been eliminated.* Distraught and in a rage, he demanded to speak with company management. Upper-level management refused to speak with Terry. Terry felt that there was a hidden agenda that he was not a part of. Due to Terry's enraged mental state, he was escorted out of the building and off the property by corporate security. Off-duty police officers were hired for the next five days to provide extra external security and ensure the safety of other employees to make sure Terry did not return to the company to harm anyone in management. With no job and very little in savings, Terry couldn't dare break the news to his wife. He told his wife a few days later that he had lost his job. His wife had a job, but only made up a fraction of the total household income. Things were looking pretty bad. As luck would have it, another critical event occurred.

With the loss of 85 percent of the household income, the couple could not afford to pay the mortgage. Murphy's Law applies here. "If it can happen, it will happen." As a result, the second thing that happened was that their home was foreclosed after 120 days of nonpayment. With no home or no job, one would think that things could not possibly get any worse. Terry had to move his family from a 4,400-square-foot home to a 950-square-foot apartment. After living in an apartment for six months, Terry realized just how much space he had in his house. Terry, his wife, and two children were literally walking on top of each other inside their very small apartment. This created frustration among all the family members. As months of unemployment went by, Terry's wife became increasingly frustrated.

As the frustration set in, Terry's wife finally decided to drop the third bomb on him. She filed for divorce. The few little assets Terry had remaining after he lost his job and his home, his wife now wanted half of that. Terry was literally having his entire manhood ripped away from him. This was just too much for him to bear. Terry had no money, no home, no job, broken up family, and soon no wife. In an attempt to salvage his life and put the pieces back together, Terry decided to do something that he had never done before. He used his knowledge, skills, and abilities to set up a criminal enterprise that put thousands of dollars in his bank account relatively quickly. This solved his short-term cash flow problem; however, law enforcement was quickly on his trail.

Terry was later arrested and convicted of money laundering and other technological crimes dealing with fraudulently accessing retirement/investment accounts. Instead of putting his faith in God and drawing strength from Him, he put his faith in something that was man-made. He put his faith in the dollar bill and thought that if he could just replace the income that he lost he would then be able to hold his family together and everything would be all right. Boy, was he wrong. Everything was not all right. His wife still divorced him. He still lost everything he owned. And to make matters worse he ran up a legal tab of about thirty thousand dollars.

I say all this to say that not one time did Terry try to refinance his home. Not one time did he seek out financial counseling to get his debt under control. Not one time did he talk to family members to let them know what was going on. I do understand that some issues remain private in a household and are not necessarily issues shared with the world. But when your back is up against the wall there are no limitations. You must seek help. Men sometimes have a problem with allowing their pride to get in the way of their progress. Not one time did he seek out spiritual guidance or turn to God for answers. Sometimes this is all God wants. He wants us to lean on Him to develop our own understanding. Terry thought he could do it all by himself and in the end he was all by himself. Sometimes if you just keep an open mind and open your ears, God sends people your way in order for you to get your break through. You must be willing to receive what God has for you and not be afraid of disappointment. Believe me when I tell you that sometimes disappointment is not a bad thing. Nobody wants to hear that they cannot have what they want when they want it. It is so important that we all learn to thank God for the things we don't have as well as for the things we do have.

Marcus Garvey was one of the first great black speakers of the twentieth century that made the black man feel like he had some dignity and life was worth living. Marcus Garvey gave several speeches to groups all over the United States stressing the importance of why black people need not depend on the system that the mainstream white America put together, but return to Africa and put together their own. Though viewed at that time as a bit of a radical, Garvey dazzled his admirers with his strong points of what the black man needed to do to be respected in the United States. The following is a partial speech given by Marcus Garvey on Easter Sunday on April 16, 1922, in Liberty Hall, New York. The title of his speech was *"The Resurrection of the Negro."* It is as follows,

The Lord is risen! A little over nineteen hundred years ago a man came to this world called Jesus. He was sent here for the propagation of a cause—that of saving fallen humanity. When he came the world refused to hear Him; the world rejected Him; the world persecuted Him; men crucified Him. A couple days ago He was nailed to a cross of Calvary; he died; He was buried. Today He is risen: risen the spiritual leader of creation; risen as the first fruit of them that slept. Today that crucified Lord, that crucified Christ, sees the affairs of man from His own spiritual throne on high.

After hundreds of years have rolled by, the doctrine He taught has become the accepted religion of hundreds of millions of human beings. He in His resurrection triumphed that His cause was spiritual. The world felt the truth about Jesus too late to have accepted His doctrine in His lifetime. But what was done to Jesus in His lifetime is just what is done too all reformers and reform movements. He came to change the spiritual attitude of man toward his brother. That was regarded in His day as an irregularity, even as it is regarded today. The one who attempts to bring about changes in the order of human society becomes a dangerous imposter upon society, and to those who control the systems of the day.

It has been an historic attitude of man to keep his brother in slavery—in subjection for the purpose of exploitation. When Jesus came the privileged few were taking advantage of the unfortunate masses. Because the teachings of Jesus sought to equalize the spiritual and even the temporal rights of man, those who held authority, sway and dominion sought His liberty by prosecution, sought His life by death. He was called to yield up that life for the cause He loved—because He was indeed a true reformer.

The example set by our Lord and Master nineteen hundred years ago is but the example that every reformer must make up his mind to follow if we are indeed to serve those to whom we minister. Service to humanity means sacrifice. That has been demonstrated by our blessed Lord and Redeemer whose resurrection we commemorate this day. As Christ triumphed nearly two thousand years ago over death and the grave, as He was risen from the dead, so do I hope that 400,000,000 Negroes of today will triumph over the slavishness of the past, intellectually, physically, morally, and even religiously; that on this anniversary of our risen Lord, we ourselves will be risen from the slumber of the ages; risen in thought to higher ideals, to a loftier purpose, to a truer conception of life.

It is the hope of the Universal Negro Improvement Association that 400,000,000 Negroes of the world will get to realize that we are about to live a new life—a risen life—a life of knowing ourselves.

How many of us know ourselves? How many of us understand ourselves? The major number of us for ages have failed to recognize in ourselves the absolute masters of our own destiny—the absolute directors and creators of our own fate.

Today as we think of our risen Lord may we not also think of the life He gave to us—the life that made us His instruments, His children—the life that He gave to us to make us possessors of the land that He himself created through His father? How many of us can reach out to that higher life; that higher purpose; that creative world that says to you, you are a man, a sovereign, a lord—lord of the creation? On this beautiful spring day, may we not realize that God made Nature for us; God has given it to us as our province, our dominion? May we not realize that God has created no superior being to us in this world, but Himself? May we not know that we are the true lords and creators of our own fate and of our own physical destiny?

Some of us seem to accept the fatalist position, the fatalist attitude, that God accorded to us a certain position and condition, and therefore there is no need trying to be otherwise. The moment you accept such an attitude, the moment you accept such an opinion, the moment you harbor such an idea, you hurl at the great God who created you, because you question Him for His love, you question Him for His mercy. God has created man, and has placed him in this world as the lord of creation, as the sovereign of everything that you see, let it be land, let it be sea, let it be the lakes, rivers, and everything therein. All that you see in creation, all that you see in the world, was created by God for the use of man, and you four hundred million black souls have as much right to your possession in this world as any other race.

Chapter 9

When All Else Fails, Keep On Trying

I am learning day by day to continually humble myself. Some of the things that we experience in life will actually take several lifetimes to understand. I don't think we are supposed to understand everything. Some things will always remain a mystery. Some things we may never be able to explain. This is where your faith is tested. I wish there was a book for parents that gives a step-by-step process on what needs to be done to raise a productive child. Unfortunately there is not one. A lot of it is trial and error. When it comes to children and child rearing, we must play the cards that are dealt to us. This is the case if you are a parent, mentor, teacher, or any position dealing with young people. The common sense approach should also never be left out. There are certain things that can be done to increase your odds one way or the other, but nothing is guaranteed. With this said, I began to understand that sometimes when you do the very best you can, it is still a possibility that you come up short. As much as I want to see every child achieve their ultimate success, I understand in the back of my mind that this is not realistic. Some kids can have the perfect upbringing with resources available to them that other kids only dream of and fail to take advantage of what they have. The tragedy in this is that valuable time is lost and can't be gotten back. Life kicks in around the age twenty-five. It seems like after the age of twenty-five, you have two birthdays a year. It seems like Christmas is every six months, and your children are growing like weeds.

For every kid that grows up in a single family household without a father and makes something of himself, there is another kid somewhere that has both parents in the home and the child is lost to the streets. As men, we must be committed to the process more so than the individual. An individual will let you down when there can be nothing at all wrong with the process. We can always figure out creative ways to improve the process hoping that more individuals are reached. But, there will always be that segment of society that will be resistant to change. That small percentage of society that no matter what is said, will not be reached. Our efforts need to be focused on the young boys and girls we do help. The way I see it, if I can just keep one child out of the backseat of my squad car, I have done my due diligence. When I'm teaching a class of twenty students about character, statistics tell me that 60 percent of them will not remember anything I said within twenty-four hours after hearing it. I would much rather have that number to decrease, but I don't get upset because I know I am reaching some of them. The way I look at it, maybe if I can get to a few of the students, maybe they will be the extra eyes and ears for the rest of the class that was not paying attention. Again, I'm committed to the process of teaching and continuing to get the word out. I'm not committed to the individual. I don't feel like I'm wasting my time. Besides, I never count the time, I make the time count. You will never know what life you may have an impact on if you are afraid of opening your mouth.

The best protection against a high-powered offense is a solid defense. When you have a solid defense, you can stop the other team from scoring. The offense in this instance is the gangbangers, drug dealers, prostitutes, hoodlums, criminals, and all the other undesirable individuals who are actively trying to recruit our boys and girls to play on their teams. Your defense should consist of education, common sense, honesty, respect, responsibility, integrity, and ethics. You can fight off any attack from the offense if you posses the correct defensive characteristics. There is an old saying, "Offense fills the stands, and defense wins the ball game." Men must keep this in mind. The bottom line is doing your best each and every time you have an opportunity to. Put forth your best efforts to help save our children. Even if they go astray, let's at least give them a fighting chance. If the defensive characteristics they need to possess are inadequate, they won't have a fighting chance at all. As parents we cannot fail at the process. If we arm our children with the essentials they need to do battle in this mean world, and later on in life they choose not to utilize what they have been taught, then the failure is on them not you. It is only on you if you have failed to train and teach. *Remember, Be The Man.*

INDEX

A

absentee parents 13, 19
Anthony (friend) 74-6
Ayanna G
    "Why Do More Black Women Attend College Than Black Men?" 64

B

Baisden, Michael 45
black community 21, 29
Brown, Lloyd 106

C

character 42, 53-4, 57
    developing our 56
Conspiracy to Destroy Black Boys, The (Kunjufu) 64
Cosby, Bill 25, 52
The Cosby Show 25

D

defense, solid 116
Digby, Joyce Marie 25
Digby, Samuel Lee, Sr. 25

*D*s of manhood, three 5, 61
dedication 71
determination 74
discipline 62, 65
DuBois, W. E. B. 63
    Souls of Black Folk, The 63
Dungy, Tony 53, 90
    Quiet Strength 90
    Uncommon 90

E

Easter 109
Easterly, Jason 95
education 32

F

family, concept of 29
Ford Motor Company 26-7

G

Gardner, Chris 61
    Pursuit of Happyness, The 61
    Start Where You Are 61
Garvey, Marcus 112
Grandma Olivee 23

Grandpa Willie Ward 23

H

Haupert, Gary 95
Hayward, Reginald 94

J

Jackson, Michael 67
   "Man in the Mirror" 67
Jacquelyn (older sister) 23, 89-90
Jordan, Michael 91
Joyce (older sister) 23-4
Juniors, Charles 95

K

Ken (friend) 74-7
King, Martin Luther, Jr. 37-8, 44, 52
   Why We Can't Wait 52
Knight, Stratton 26
Kunjufu, Jawanza 64
   Conspiracy to Destroy Black Boys, The 64
Kunkle, David 68

L

laziness 25, 45-6
leadership, effective 105-6
Liebow, Elliott 51
   Talley's Corner 51
love, mother's 30

M

management, effective 106
Manske, Fred 106
   Secrets of Effective Leadership 106
McNabb, Donovan 94

men, types of 84
   first 84
   second 85
   third 85
mind, child's 30

P

parenting 13, 15
prayer, childhood 31
Pride, Dan 109
projects, funding for community 36
Purpose Driven Life, The (Warren) 34
Pursuit of Happyness, The (Gardner) 61

Q

Quiet Strength (Dungy) 90

R

reputation 57
Robinson, Kenneth 107-8
Robinson, Marilyn 107

S

Secrets of Effective Leadership (Manske) 106
Shannon (younger brother) 23
sheet, hot 20
Souls of Black Folk, The (Dubois) 63
Start Where You Are (Gardner) 61
success 99
   plan 99
   vision 100

T

Talley's Corner (Liebow) 51
teacher, law enforcement 38

technology 103-4
Terry (friend) 110-12
Tolliver, Juan 108
tombstone courage 11-13
Torian, Reginald 95

U

Uncommon (Dungy) 90
United States, changes in the 37
Universal Negro Improvement Association 114
Up from Slavery (Washington) 90
UPS 96-7

V

victim of a crime 79-80

W

Ward, Willie 28
Warren, Rick
  Purpose Driven Life, The 34
Washington, Booker T. 90
  Up from Slavery 90
Washington, Herb 95
"Why Do More Black Women Attend College Than Black Men?" (Ayanna G) 64
Why We Can't Wait (King) 52

Edwards Brothers,Inc!
Thorofare, NJ 08086
01 Aug, 2010
BA2010213